UNAPOLOGETICALLY YOU

FREEDOM TO BE

CHANTELLE BECKING

LIFEWISE BOOKS

UNAPOLOGETICALLY YOU
FREEDOM TO BE
Chantelle Becking

Published by:

⚙️LIFEWISE BOOKS

PO BOX 1072
Pinehurst, TX 77362
LifeWiseBooks.com

To contact the author: chantellebecking.com

ISBN (Print): 978-1-947279-67-4

ISBN (Ebook): 978-1-947279-68-1

DEDICATION

To all dreamers—never stop the pursuit of all the things. The world will tell you it is not reasonable...God will remind you to NEVER live reasonably.

If you can dream it, don't let anyone tell you it can't be done. That's between you and God. If people think your dream is ludicrous, you are likely right on track.

A LITTLE BIG LOVE MOMENT FOR MY PEOPLE

Beck: You are the man and by that, I mean THE man. No one else in the world would hang on for this wild ride with me. We are in this together.

My girls Bianca, Solie, Ari, Dolly, & Lennyx: You are fierce little warriors. Thanks for teaching me every day to be brave and for believing mom can do all things. You keep me dreaming and doing.

My mom and sister: You are everything. I have no better or bigger words. We have walked through fire together and lived to hug it all out.

My girlfriends: You know who you are you. Bad-to-the-bone women who light the world on fire. I am so proud to do life with you. Radical, crazy dreams and simple kayaking days. It all matters.

Photo creds: Sheri Grippo-Cabral: The talent behind every image that is shot of our family. You get it. You are all heart and soul and your Bible flips have moved mountains in my life.

And to all of those who have loved and supported me when everyone else thought I should be committed…you know who you are.

Let's get to it!

CONTENTS

INTRODUCTION
'CAUSE LORD KNOWS 40,000 WORDS ARE NOT ENOUGH

Not so long ago, I was being wheeled back on a gurney for the biggest leap of faith God has ever called me to. *How in the world did I get to this place?* My mind was spinning. I have yet to find the words. I was scared to death and yet had peace like I had never experienced in my life; a total oxy-moron, right?

I start great books but never finish them. Maybe it's my five kids that keep me semi-distracted. It could be my complete lack of organization or tendency to overcommit. Maybe I feel guilty— hello woman guilt—thinking I should be reading my Bible instead of whatever I have to do at the moment. It seems the older I get, the less I seem to remember stuff, like scripture and the appropriate times and places to pick up my children.

Girls, we need freedom. I need freedom, and this book is a little window into the journey I am taking to get there. I have had monumental highs and crawl-under-the-couch embarrassing lows. I share a good deal of them with you, right here in these pages mainly because I want to pull the curtain back on real lives we are actually living instead of those we snap and filter on social media.

My hope is that parts of this book are YES GIRL, YES! And others you can skim. You might feel like my life is all adoption and foster care based…well, that is not a lie. But I can tell you, it all applies the same- just wrapped up a teensy bit different. We all have our wild journeys. If we were completely honest, no one would truly believe them. That's also my hope—that we become completely honest. Freedom is a journey I am on and NO, sister, I am not there yet, but I hope we will get there together one day.

A warning to my lovies: Listen, I love Jesus. He is my Ultimo Homie. I will also likely have a few savory words that might mess with a few of you as you skim along this ditty. Please know, I would not use them if they were not a part of who I am. I guess I am a little rough around the edges. I have always believed that all words paint a picture and sometimes the picture is a little messy, and maybe even PG-13, and possibly stuck like an unfortunate piece of toilet paper to a gal's stilettos when she thinks she is really rocking it.

I hope you can give my words some grace if you are easily offended. Shock value is occasionally needed to get the point across (in my humble opinion, which you will likely find it is actually not all that humble). I am pretty blunt with my language. I am on a voyage. I am not quite there yet, and I guess I feel like I have to write the book as myself instead of the girl I might think you need me to be.

I have committed to just be me. That is not as easy as I thought it would be. I have started to really dig in to allow people to see my not-so-shiny parts. I have lived a series of less than stellar moments. I have spent year after year searching, only to find I can just be regular old fabulously jacked up me.

We live a lot of life more like a highly filtered version of our real-life selves. It is like coming home after a long night at a fancy gig. You know, the kind of evening you think about and possibly dread for months. It means doing the hair, makeup, the shaving of the legs way up past the knee, and typically Spanx. It is all a façade, this get up. No matter what size I am prior to said event, I feel the need to torture myself. *Let's just mash down that belly gut a teensy bit more.* It is a straitjacket, security blanket kind of deal for my tortured mind.

Stay with me, girls...

You know at the end of one of those evenings where all the dancing has happened, and your feet feel like you just did a fire walk? The kind of night your toes have been stuffed like sausages in a fabulous pair of shoes for three hours too long?

There is no sweeter freedom than coming home. It is like I imagine it would feel being released from prison after a spell. Off come the fake eyelashes, face paint, the shoes, the dress...and finally the girdle-y torture chamber. If you have never worn Spanx, well bless your heart. But if you have, you know the sweet bliss of release that follows when the body escapes all that nonsense and restriction.

Well, this book is kind of like that. We can present life quite nicely. I can smile and nod and deliver one boss of a smoke and mirror show, but that won't really help anyone get free. So, I promise to share the good, the bad, and the ugly. Even that sounds like a load because although I know I just need to BE, sometimes I don't. I hop right back on that hamster wheel trying to earn my way into God's good graces along with my kids and husband and whoever needs me at the moment. Don't believe the lie. We are all just trying to figure it out, not let anyone down, and keep spinning the many plates simultaneously.

Maybe life has left you feeling tired, let down, duped, guilty, discouraged, disillusioned…same here, some days. This book is not meant to fix all the stuff. I wrote it to help us all feel a bit more visible…if you feel like you are fading and need to get your "Towanda" back. (If you have no clue about Towanda, congratulations on being young. Check out the 1990's movie *Fried Green Tomatoes.*)

From a distance, another's life seems almost perfect, but it never is. I have been torn down and built back up over and over again. It is a constant process, isn't it? It has been one hell of a life so far, even with the bumps and bruises. Every single one of my life choices and disasters God actually used for good. So, have hope, dear soul.

We get to choose to be conquerors of our pain and past. There really is no stopping us. So here is to getting a little TOWANDA! every day.

Well, don't just sit there. Lean in!

CHAPTER 1
THIS IS US—AND STUFF

Well, here we are. This is my family. This is my life. I am Momma to five girls. Now, before you think there is no way you can relate to a woman who has five kids, hang in here. My life goal was not to do this…but God. We were an unlikely match, all of us. Funny how life works. I was so sure I would not have kids for many years. I loved the thrill of the corporate world and dang, we had a lot of fun before the tiny humans. Then God moved our hearts and adoption happened.

Out of what seemed like nowhere, I was a parent. MOM - That title took a while to get used to. Before I was a mom, the last thing I wanted to hear about was every single detail about someone else's kid. Oh, that is actually a good note to self. *Reminder to self: Don't bore people with stuff about my posse of kids.* Good luck.

We are a mostly happy tribe of seven. Eight, if you count Marley, the best dog in the world. *Trust me on this one. I have tested several other canine beings.* If you are looking at the group of us wondering how the heck this all came together...same here. Sometimes life takes you on a wild ride that seems to happen in the blink of an eye, while simultaneously feeling like a lifetime.

Pictures, especially family photos, can present themselves as little white lies or at least tiny fibs. Are we happy? Mostly, yes. But are we also totally messed up in ways I could never express appropriately in written word? Also, yes. Good thing I have a super fab photog bestie who can airbrush most of our grit away.

I don't know about you, but I always like to get a feel for a girl when I meet her. I wonder what her life is like and what I can expect from her. So, in that vein, I will give you a little insight into my life. Here is a snapshot of what to expect if you were to randomly show up at our compound:

Our home-life is typically lived loud. Music is playing nonstop. Dancing is happening on Momma's good days. No one can seem to find the remote. The dog is barking. The kids are pile driving each other. All major kitchen surfaces are sticky. Somehow my kids talked us into putting a full-size trampoline in our fireplace room over Christmas, soooo you can guess what that is like on a day-to-day basis. Also, on a total side note, what the heck happens when you jump on a trampoline after forty? Uh, why exactly did NO ONE tell me I would randomly and uncontrollably pee? It's weird.

We have to be more honest, ladies. I could have bypassed loads of embarrassment if I had been given a head's up. Is it just when I jump? *Yes.* It is also when I try to do a non-stretchy version of an old cheerleading move? Apparently also *yes.* Thanks, friends. Or maybe I should say to you…*You are welcome.* At least I love you enough to forewarn you.

On a regular day, if I don't know you are stopping by, there might be the faintest smell of pee. Now hang on…it is not mine, which might be confusing after my overshare trampoline reveal.

I am trying to set you up with full honesty here, so this is a bitty baby step in that direction. I think little kid pee or possibly temporary loaner dog pee has gotten in weird places I have not been notified of… eeek. Don't even ask me why. I cannot locate it! It used to drive me nuts, but I have kind of accepted it in a wamp-wamp sort of way.

We took in a small boy dog for a while who was a leg hiker. I guess you can figure out how quickly he found a more suitable home. Still, I figure that life is short, and one of my tribe is likely doing something I had rather not know the details of in our humble abode. I hate to admit it, but there are marker and crayon art displays on too many of our walls. (I swore that would never be me!) Luckily, I am raising teensy Picassos. *Yeah, for sure. That is totally what's happening.* There are also suckers stuck underneath the couch cushions with a landmine of goldfish.

Uh…back to your visit.

We are all booked up at our home sweet home these days. When we bought it, we had no clue we would have so many children. Go ahead and bring a sleeping bag when you visit 'cause there ain't much room left at The Becking Inn. If I don't know you are coming, you might walk in the door that is almost never truly closed, only to randomly find me trying to take a bathroom break alone (which also won't be happening).

Why exactly do they refer to it as a RESTroom anyway? I am not resting in there in any form or fashion. When I go to the toilet, my kids…all five…seem to have their best ideas or need all the world's problems solved. There is no escaping it since none of the locks work on any of our doors. That's what happens when life is like a tornado and someone is always locking themselves in rooms that they have no business being in alone. Hence, all the broken locks. So, if you want to get a good picture of us, think of a Chip and JoAnna Gaines kind of home and then go a full throttle 180. That should suit us nicely.

Now, if I do know you are coming, I will completely freak out. So actually, you probably shouldn't visit. Maybe we should just text. I would say call, but that is ludicrous. Everyone knows I do not use the real-life phone unless it is a 911 situation. And even in that situation…*hello*…texting would be best.

We don't have many real-life visitors for so many reasons. But if you must come, I want you to feel loved, so I am gonna lose my stinking mind trying to clean up before you get here. My kids probably won't love you at first but don't take it personally. It is more a reflection of me. Prior to your arrival, I will likely use some voices that include hollering and give some very firm direction to motivate the mini-me's to get the house semi-presentable.

We will shove stuff in places I will not find for months to come, but it will look semi-decent if you give me a seven-day heads up. And don't worry, I will have that urine stench camouflaged with some sort of smell good that takes your breath away…literally.

Life seems to move fast when there are so many people under one roof. So, now that you feel right at home as I ramble on about my life, I think it would be a good idea to give you some words to plug in, to connect with each of these five adorable cherubs you are going to get to know sporadically throughout these pages.

Here is how it plays out kid-wise:

Bianca, debuted back in 2006

- Oldest Sister. Runs the household better than her momma
- Responsibly wonderful Type A
- Lover of all things slime and please stay out of her room

- She loves momma except when she doesn't
- Back handspring master
- Guatemalan princess

Solie, rolled into being 2009

- Triple threat
- Set to replace Beyonce in another ten years
- Ethiopian delight
- Never had a bad day in her life
- Too legit to quit.
- The future famous one, no doubt

Ari, started her world tour back in 2011

- Mischievous charmer
- Crafty as all get out
- Chess playing savant
- Overcomer
- Leader of the pack for the little sisters
- Whatever happened…she DID NOT DO IT
- Acts tough, but is a total softy

Delia (Dolly), started stealing all of the hearts in 2013

- Cuteness overload
- She gets exactly what she wants
- Heart as big as the sea
- Kisses and hugs one thousand times a day, but don't cross her

Lennyx, unexpectedly changed the world with her tiny self back in 2015

- Baby boss
- Do all the things she asks, and do them right now, so no one gets hurt
- Ultimate baby, that's not actually a baby. But because she is the youngest of the family, she runs the complete show
- Lover of Chumpy Charms (That is Lucky Charms to the over-three crowd)
- Unexpected game changer for this mom's life

Eric Becking (Beck)

- Ultimo Dad/Hubs extraordinaire
- You guys…he has five daughters…you know he is a boss in all areas related to little girls
- Lover of Chuck Taylors—Converse to the lay person
- Creator of #ChuckTaylorTuesday (Learn about this #WALKINLOVE movement)
- If you need motivation, he is your guy
- The favorite parent by a landslide
- I like him a lot, too

Marley

- Best dog in all the land
- Goldendoodle dandy
- Pommeled daily by the little kids and totally rolls with it
- Stealer of all food not highly managed

Chantelle (Me)

- Lover of coffee, tattoos, and Jesus
- I like more stuff, I just thought those made me sound cooler
- Wordsmith
- Nonstop sing-talker and talk out loud to myself, kinda gal
- Obsessed with hats…Bring them all to me
- Below-average dancer but uber confident in my moves
- Known consistently as the "inappropriate friend"
- Enneagram #8 but kinda wish I was…who am I kidding …I'm an #8

That is a snapshot of the Becking Tribe. While it might seem like I am complaining at times about random tribemates during this book (I probably am), please note, we are full of love and maybe occasionally teetering on the edge of insanity.

#MomLife

One step of faith led me (of all people) to become a mom. The plans I had in my head for my life have turned out pretty much the opposite. I went from power suits and "Please do not sit anyone with a kid next to me on the plane," to #momlife. I still don't feel like a mom some days. I know that must sound nuts but 'tis real. Mom of one soon became two and then entered into the world of foster care; another avenue I was not planning. I don't know if you can relate to that or not, (not necessarily the foster care thing, just the life avenue thing). Some days as I am driving around in my big, sticky, kid-crusted-up suburban picking up all the humans, I wonder how I got here.

Maybe I am having an overachieving day, all the makeup and the outfit on paired with non-sensible shoes. Because, friends, I love shoes. It starts okay. We pace ourselves just trying to load all humans into the bus, baby steps I say. Keep my mind in the "ohm" position. It's very Zen of me. Sweet talk and encouragement soon enough morphs into a clenched teeth hostile negotiation with a toddler only to finish loading the little screamers while I am covered in stress sweat. Namaste, y'all.

Pride has been my downfall, even down to driving a minivan. I said I would never do it. I still don't, but I should. I am 45, and loading kids in and out of that suburban thingy makes me work up a lather. Not so long ago, I had three in car seats. I guess you can imagine the totally relaxing process that it was to load and unload, in the summer especially. What in the holy hell are car seat manufacturers thinking? I mean, are there only old-ish men creating these things?

I can just imagine their think tank now:

Let's get a 42-point harness system. Yes. Definitely. Oh! How about-all the buckles? Bring them all! And for fun, let's make the car seat weigh more than the one installing it. Also, lets create lots of nooks and crannies for crumbs and foul milk to collect. That seems fair. Then let's giggle like school girls as we watch one mom wrangle and bribe all her little critters to enter the car and begin the process to safely contain them in the rare case they might actually be launched into outer space. No worries, they aren't going anywhere!

I am not positive this is how car seats came about... but I am pretty sure that's it in a nutshell.

Same Same

Do you ever wonder how your life got to this place? Uh-huh.

Ever feel alone?

Empty?

Tired?

Lost?

Same.

Bloated?

Addicted to Carbs?

Yearning for more and unsure where to start?

Then this book is for you *and* me!

My world might have kids crawling all over it, but girlfriend, we are the same. Probably not all around the same, hence all these kids. But in our quest for the good life, for more, we just might have a lot in common. I mean we might be packaged totally different, but we share some of the same stuff. I might be a bit more outspoken than you. Or you might have better manners than me, but we have both lived life. Maybe you feel nothing at all, like life is just happening and you are a spectator in your own world. I have been there too, sister, and that one might be the toughest of all.

Life is no joke. I have yet to meet anyone without some battle scars. I mean, we can all play a good game pretending to have it all together, but the blissful liberation comes when we kind of let it all go. Kiss that game goodbye.

My life has been a series of pushing limits. Wow, that sentence makes me sound like a bad to the bone biker chic, which is awesome, but not totally true. Mostly the limits are pushed with God, I guess. Luckily, He has all this grace, which I am completely thrilled about, because I need a heap of it daily.

If only we could see people's real-life stories in pictures. Wow! Social media would be a much different beast. As women, we tend to be so hard on ourselves. We open up the "Facebooks", as we refer to it in our house, zone out, and stare at all those seemingly perfect families. *Look at her. See her family's new stuff. Her kids are so smart. They won yet another award. Her house is so clean, and her hair is always fixed, and I bet she and her husband make out all of the time.*

I feel more and more like crap about how average I am. You know the drill. (It is a lie, y'all!)

While I love a superfly, photoshopped version of us, for the most part, we are fairly solid in being just a big old mess. Our family is kind of an enigma, I guess. I have tried so hard to live the other way and it is too tiring. Trying to act perfect is too hard. Oh, I know that does not sound the least bit sexy to a reader. Maybe that is a bad use of the word there. And maybe I am lying to myself. Maybe I totally just want to act like we are *so fine* with ourselves and our life, and that I never worry about how cool everyone else is. Yeah, that's probably more accurate.

Maybe you wonder why the heck I am writing a book. Me too, some days. I am over here wondering why you are reading it. I guess for the most part God has had it on my heart for some time. Funny how good things can actually be used for bad. I have some of my most favorite authors I look up to so much. I read all of their stuff or at least the first three chapters and wonder how they became such great communicators. They started. Period. Like me and you, one day they decided their story might help someone else, so they conjured up enough chutzpah and put pen to paper.

> I spent a solid 30–35 years convinced I was not enough. I played small when I knew better in my soul. I covered up just a tiny part of what helped me breathe easy. I have been bold, don't get me wrong, but there are pockets of my life where I have lived in constant fear of being judged.

I have a past. It haunts me occasionally though I have gotten some serious redemption. Sometimes we look at other women who seem to have it together and imagine their lives. I promise you they are never as they seem.

Who We Are vs. Who People Think We Are

I am always blown away when I meet someone for the first time that only knows my family from afar. Clearly, they don't read what I write about or they would know exactly how far from perfect we are. They see us on a random good day when most of us have bathed and a few of the kids are wearing matching socks. Looks are deceiving, friends. Yes, we showed up at church as a family unit. Yes, that was also me screaming at the top of my lungs, "Get in the damn car or else!" just before we left the house. Clearly, Momma needs Jesus. We look at each other. We assume so much from afar, but a closer, real-life look into another's life typically reveals something we can all relate with…*flaws*.

I am drenched in flaws. It is great to be able to admit it, but it is also our responsibility to do something about it. I will tell you I have been an amazing friend and wife and also a crappy one. Most of the time my intentions have been good, but my mouth gets me in a world of hurt. I have had to learn and lose. And by that, I mean people in my life. Sometimes our strengths are also our biggest weaknesses. So, while I am confident in being a truth teller, I can also hurt people with my words in pursuit of my truthfulness. There is a fine line there that I am learning to navigate. So, keep in mind as you read along, this girl needs grace.

Who Cares?

Let me help you get unchained for one second. When we worry about what others think about us, we are wasting our own time. The people God gives us will love us unconditionally. There will always be people around who judge us. It will happen, and it will continue to happen. It is human nature. Imagine all of the time we spend in life worried about what someone else might say about us. How many lunches and dinner parties and play dates have we sat through knowing these are not our people?

I see that hand. Yes! Too many.

It is time to stop the nonsense and get to living. We cannot expect anyone else…hear me girls…ANYONE…to totally get what God has called us to. I hope it looks radical and bonkers and totally out of the norm. Praise Him! I can promise it is not going to look safe and comfortable and work well with others' ideas of normal. Don't we know by now God wants to blow the doors off normal? Plus, when we get perspective, who wants to live an average life?

Geez, that sounds exciting. I don't want my eulogy to wrap up with, "She was a sweet, people pleasing lady who lived a kind and ordinary life." Uh…check please. I want my going away party to be a situation where people who love me come around and think, "How the heck are we going to wrap this up in words?"

"She was radical for God and lived on the edge!" I don't know, maybe that's a start.

We are meant for anything but average. Maybe you have an average job or marriage or singleness or living situation. You get to decide to step out of your comfort zone and get to it. Get to living. Days, weeks, and months can slip by in the spin of the hamster wheel. It happens. We can refocus. Ask God what He wants to do in our lives and expect Him to answer. Always. I want to challenge you and myself to LIVE. Serve others selflessly in the midst of your pain and all of a sudden, your trials seem a little smaller.

Come On Now

So, no more living in fear. We get to baby step it together. It is a journey. Fear is a liar, friends. It is stealing our lives. What if we decided to wake up and attack fear? I guarantee I would get much more beauty rest. Our options are limitless when there is no fear involved. Think of the examples we set for our kids, our girls.

What if we raised a generation of girls who were warriors, comfortable in their own skin? Confident in their choices, settling for nothing. Talk about a takeover. If you are a momma reading this, I am talking straight talk to you, sister. We must get about this in our own lives if we want this for our girls or our boys who will marry girls. So many of us will do anything in the world for our kids but not for ourselves. I want to tell you, that needs to stop. We must invest in ourselves. God has a plan for us. Of course, our kids are important. Yes, but so are we.

> If we want to raise our kids to be fierce in the right ways, we must model the same thing in our own lives.

We are daughters of the King and its time we started to act like it. I have gone 'round and 'round with this term over the past year or so. I grew up with a twisted-up view of God and I am still not sure it is totally on track. I have always battled the thoughts of God seeing me as a disappointment. Or when I screw up, thinking He is so mad at me or I will never be enough.

If we have pains with our earthly fathers, it can so translate to our view of God. *Maybe He will leave us. Maybe He will move on and forget us. I will never measure up.* The list goes on, but the answer is NO! He wants the world for us. Daughters of The Freaking King! My next tattoo right there. These words are legit. Everything. Royalty. It doesn't mean there will be no pain. It does mean He is forever in our corner, loving us and wanting us to succeed. He wants joy for us.

I hope you take this journey with me. I am writing this for both of us. I am just a regular girl. I feel the same fears you feel. I worry about some of the same stuff you worry about. I miss out on opportunities because I am scared sometimes. I don't want to miss anything though. I want to see what is out there for me. I want to live free. And when I mess it up, I want the courage to know tomorrow is another day and I get to wake up and get a go at being awesome all over again.

CHAPTER 2
GET TO STEPPIN'

The struggle is happening for all of us. As much as I do not love seeing my physical body age, I freaking love the freedom that comes in my mind with age. I want to say how I have matured, but I am not sure that it's the right use of words. The things I cared about so much before are a distant memory now in many areas. I have friends, like real, solid, hide a body in the trunk of their car if needed, kind of friends. The number is a lot lower than it was in previous years, but I never have to second guess a conversation or wonder if I get grace when I am ridiculous in my words. It is understood. If I say many things that seem too blunt and often inappropriate, they know it. They love me in spite of me at times and are not afraid to tell me to slow my roll.

My girlfriends have been there to keep me grounded, or at least in one place. I'm a life-long runner, and I don't mean the kind that needs a pair of running shoes. I could start just about anywhere in my life and see that there is a very common strain. I run. Not as much now as my earlier years when my face and booty were both significantly tighter.

Sidebar: If you are reading this and you are currently rocking your twenties, enjoy your firm caboose. Please, do it for me. Actually, do it for all of us who have misplaced our backsides with age. Put the book down right now and get in front of a full-length mirror and appreciate your bootie for what it is. No, seriously, I mean do that right now. You will thank me later. I know, it is hard to really wrap your head around this request. All you have known is a tight back side. Bless you. I am living vicariously through you right this second.

A Quick PSA on Stuff You Likely Don't Want to Know About Me

I can only speak for myself and millions of other women when I say, something happens back there, the backside. I was in denial for so long. It wasn't until my oldest daughter laid a truth bomb on me when I had to face the fact that my rear had slid into my legs. One day I was rocking those skinny jeans, and in a blink, they were sliding down my bum. *What in the world?* Maybe it was because I totally quit exercising for a few years, but mostly it was the dreaded aging butt slide. I don't know what was harder to accept, the loss of my bootie or the way it had settled down so low on the back of my legs. Like one day it just gave up. If it could speak, it might say,

"Hey girl, I am tired. I will be down here if you need me. My work is done."

Of course, I am all Zen with aging, you know. Not a care in the world over here. I have accepted all of the things about aging…just keep the Botox handy. A few years ago, I totally stopped shaving my legs past the knee cap. Take that, Mother Nature! Fist pump emoji. I was tired mostly. All of the requirements of woman life were getting put on the back burner while I tried to just get up and live day to day.

My act of rebellion randomly caught up with me when a swanky event popped up. Somehow the upper leg, although it does not grow as much hair these days, seemed to grow very long hairs randomly that were not good to look at paired with a fabulous shorty dress. I had it all going on, at least in my mind, until I got to the event where the bright lights revealed I could likely make a small braid out of the hair on the back of my legs. Oh well, it makes me relatable, right? No? Maybe not.

I need to rethink this one, but somehow the same thing keeps happening to me. I hope that is not a sign of dementia. Ugh. I can't remember stuff. *Now, what was I talking about?* I am constantly calling everyone I see "friend". Hey, friend who is fabulous, I am sure, I totally recognize your face and have zero clue on your name. That is a friend alright? Sometimes, I switch it up with "sister" or "momma" or "girlfriend," but I don't pull off "girlfriend" very successfully.

Remember when "hot mess" was the buzz word? I could not do it. I wanted to be hip and stuff, but I just sounded like a fool saying it. I do quite well making a fool of myself on my own without trying to kill it in the buzz word department. Just wait though. I am going to try to work "hot mess" into this book some way, somehow. Wow, you just learned a whole bunch of stuff that happens in my head, and on my legs apparently.

Back to the Actual Story

I look back at my life and wonder how I got to my mid-forties. I have arm wrestled God for so many of those forty plus years. I have always had a string of fierceness and because of that, control is what I seem to be drawn to no matter what I learn or how much God has shown me that I have no actual control.

I married super young. I had no clue what I wanted to do in life. I was 23. I had a good job, but I always felt insecure for not finishing college. I am not sure if I felt the need for a degree or the guilt was just high from failing out time and time again due to my rebellious nature. I didn't feel smart. That is outrageous but true. Actually, it makes me feel sad for my younger self even thinking about it now. I needed a self-esteem hug, I guess. I acted so confident. I finished a vo-tech school and became a respiratory therapist after crashing and burning (repeatedly) in my college attempts.

I cannot believe all the responsibility I would take on in my job working in the ICU at a local hospital. I loved it. It was not what I wanted to do with my life, but I loved the rush of adrenaline. I loved helping people and making decisions in high stress situations. A few years later, I married Eric. We decided we wanted to work together which I highly UN-recommend. I gave up my job and relocated.

Working With the Hubs...

We took a spin on the student ministry wheel. It was not for us. I guess growing up I kind of thought that if I really wanted to follow God, I would need to be in full time ministry. What a lesson I learned. I was miserable trying to rally high school students for Jesus. Eric was my counterpart leading these students and we were both way out of our league. It did not last long. We were newly married and feeling all of the awkwardness of meshing our lives together. It was painful.

> God nudges me. Typically, when I ask, He responds. A good deal of the time, His response is not what I am looking for.

So, I go it alone. This is what happened just a few years after our go at student ministry. We had moved several times; first, from small town Missouri to Chicago, then to San Diego. I loved San Diego with my everything, but something was not right. We never quite found a groove. I had a bad church experience and Eric and I seemed to be growing apart. After a few years, we were at a crossroads. Eric had to decide on his future career since there was, at the time, a lack of one. He was the one with a college degree after all. (I held it against him just a smidge.)

Neither of us had a clue what we wanted in life. I gave him an ultimatum to "figure it out or else". (I mentioned I am good at running, right?) Through a series of twists and turns, he found chiropractic. He knew this was the path for him. He had known most of his life God had given him the gift of healing and he had always been a no medicine kind of guy. Great! He found his deal. Wahoo. Now, he only had to go back to school for almost five years to be able to practice. Huh? This was not my plan. Nevertheless, we packed up and moved back to St. Louis. This time I decided I would go for one of my goals too, a college degree. My parents were amazing. I know they had to be wondering if I would ever get my life together, but my dad (the one who raised me and loved me through all of life's stuff—not bio, but the real deal) told me he would help me finish college. I was thrilled.

Learning to Skedaddle

I had the luxury of going to a very progressive university. I was blown away by how much I felt like I was in the right place. I had been there for one year when a professor of mine pulled me aside and challenged me to consider studying abroad. I had never let that cross my mind. Study abroad? Thailand? Hmmm. I was not even sure I knew exactly where Thailand was on the map. That wonderful Jewish woman planted a seed within me that day that changed my life.

At first, I thought there was no way I could do it. I was married after all. I immediately went to talk to Eric's mom about it. I knew she would be honest and obviously she had his best interest in mind. To my surprise, she said I should totally do it. Of course, I have told you already a little about how right on Eric is. He has never—not even one time—shut me down from doing anything. So, sister, if you are on the market and looking for a man, find someone like this guy. We talk ourselves out of a thousand things. We women don't need a partner based in fear.

Eric was on board. Just a few months later, I was boarding a plane solo to a country where I knew exactly two words of the language. I really had no idea what was in store. What could happen in three months anyway? If only…

THESE ARE WORDS GOD TOLD ME TO PUT RIGHT HERE IN CASE YOU ARE SKIMMING:

Even when we run blatantly away from the life God is calling us to, He is still in control. He has grace, and He loves us the same. His love for us NEVER changes no matter what we do to screw it up.

I Kept Running—A Lot Like Forrest Gump

Running seems to be my theme. I have spent years getting way off track, while God's theme in my life seems to be one of mostly loving me through it and pulling me back in. Don't get me wrong, I have had to pay for some of my ridiculous choices from the distant and not so distant past. It didn't happen that I just got fixed and now I am all better. It is a continuous challenge in my life to follow God and not my own selfish ambition.

Back to Thailand…while there, I decided I would study Buddhism and basically put my faith in God on hold. You might need to re-read that. Poor choice number 12,343. As we traveled and spent time at various monasteries, we had to take on the practices of the monks. It was beautiful and mind boggling all at once. While I was trying to fast track enlightenment, I was drifting everywhere else. My marriage was hanging by a thread. Thousands of miles between two people can do that. I was doing all kinds of things in a far-away domain that could have landed me in a Thai prison. It was a very strange and dark time. Over and over, I ran. Over and over, God protected me.

One night, I left my group at a remote monastery after feeling like I would explode if I had one more hour of silence and meditation 'cause (spoiler alert) I run. I was not trying to think about my actual life choices at the moment. I got on a train in the middle of nowhere. I could read exactly none of the signs and there were no English subtitles conveniently written…anywhere. My stubbornness quickly turned to fear. I was scared. I was really scared. It was not exactly a time of iPhones with locator systems built in. I was alone. No one on earth knew where I was, and I had no idea if I was headed in the right direction.

A few trains later, I was able to get back to the little fishing village where I was living. It was 3 a.m. when I stepped off the train. I looked around nervously while trying to act like I knew what was up. No tuk tuks (Thai scooter taxis) in sight.

I saw three men asleep on their motorcycles. These were my options. I could not walk to my place. It was too far. I had to summon my courage right about then, and don't you know it, I reached out to God. I had been praying a bit on the trains. I still was trying to do it on my own, but the second I stepped off the train back into my village, I knew I was taking a risk bigger than I had before. This was a safe place by day. By night, a girl like me could disappear and no one would have a clue. I knew by then how to say my address and negotiate baht (payment) in Thai. Inside, I was freaking out.

I chose the guy that looked the least dangerous, which sounds funny as I write about it, but I remember looking so closely at each of their faces. It took a second for me to rouse him from his apparent slumber. He was a huge guy and his motorcycle seemed to barely hold him let alone me on the back with my giant backpack. I was sure I could outrun him, if needed. I got on the back of his motorcycle wondering where in the world I would end up. There I was, half way around the world in the middle of the night. I was on the back of a motorcycle with a complete stranger, who I had to wake up. Really, I was just doing a bang-up job on life choices right about then.

Life was going on as usual in the states. I was so glad Eric and my parents did not have a looking glass view into where I was at that moment. I prayed nonstop as I hung on to that driver. I could not quite get my arms all the way around his belly and frequently, we hit potholes. Several times I thought I would fall off the back from the weight of my pack. It felt like we drove for days. In all reality it was about fifteen minutes. We arrived. I paid him and ran like hell. What in the world was I doing? The reality of just how serious the situation could have become hit me once I got back to my room. There I was in total and complete rebellion, and God was there with His eye on me. I am sure He was thinking, "*Bless her heart. She is a stubborn one.*" I am guessing God's thoughts would be PG rated…a lot less like mine at the time.

That trip changed my life for so many reasons. Overall, the Thai people were wonderful and I learned so much respect for living in another culture. I mastered squat peeing and eluding rats the size of cats. I experimented (to put it gently) and saw things I could never verbalize. I was changed. I realized I loved seeing how another part of the world lived. I had been so sheltered. And now I felt like I could take on the world. I decided to do just that and maybe possibly bring God along for the ride…I mentioned my issue with pride, right? Don't even think I was about to get that sorted out.

A Dream is There for a Reason

I had one year left of studies before the elusive degree was in hand. It was a huge accomplishment for me, and I was on a mission to see and experience the world. Meanwhile, Eric was in chiropractic school with another few years left. Once I graduated, it was back to real life with a real big girl job. Eric planted a seed about six months before I graduated, after seeing the passion I had for travel. He encouraged me. If I had somewhere else I wanted to go, I needed to get to it.

I started researching on the old school dial up internet every night (y'all, it was like 2002). I knew I was supposed to go to Africa. I had no idea why. I had no clue even what countries were there, but I was meant to go. I spent night after night for months just trying to email anyone I could find with a nonprofit who would let me go there and stay with them. It was not like today where everyone has a website and all things are at your fingertips. This was a lot of years ago. Months into my research I finally had a woman email me back. Uganda. That would be my first stop. As the time passed, I also found an option in Kenya and South Africa. My trip was planned.

We Think We Know

One of my long-time girlfriends decided she would join me for the first leg of the trip. Talk about an adventure! I thought Thailand was a stretch. Landing in Africa was surreal; however, I knew I was meant to be there. I was still searching. I was on and off with God, mostly off, I suppose. I was so sure He would ask me to do something I hated with my life. I could not have been more wrong.

I arrived at the woman's orphanage in Jinja, Uganda. An orphanage. How unlikely. I had never particularly been a kid person, but this was the person's place who replied to my email…so there I was.

The next few weeks were blaringly eye opening on so many levels. There in the midst all of the culture shock and chaos, I stumbled onto my purpose. There was a sick baby room at the orphanage. It was not really popular with volunteers or workers because some of the babies were very ill. It smelled bad and it was the darkest room in the place. There was only one window, so the air (which was bad enough anyway) was extra stale from lack of ventilation. There was an overall depression surrounding it.

I walked in one day to see a baby girl in need of a breathing treatment. Hey, that was my jam. I had been a respiratory therapist. I could totally get her set up. Baby Sharon grabbed my heart and yanked it right out of my chest that day. I was caught off guard. Up until that point, I was very comfortable in life thinking mostly about myself. There was something about baby Sharon that was magical in the midst of her dire situation. I spent the next three weeks with her in that dark room.

It was in that sad little room where I started to pray again, mostly for baby Sharon. I looked for new ways to help her situation though I knew she would likely not make it. She had been forgotten, not once but repeatedly. Being dropped at the orphanage was a loss, but the bigger loss happened on a daily basis. They were radically understaffed. Children were being left at the gate daily. The American who ran the orphanage had long lost her heart for her mission, likely due to the overwhelming needs that could never seem to be met. Her heart had hardened. At the time I really judged her, but now I realize she was doing what she could. The stress of it all was too much to bear.

Game Changed

I fell in love in the dark smelly room in the back of the orphanage grounds. It was so hot and muggy and there was intermittent electricity. The flies were horrible and because Baby Sharon was weak, she had no energy to keep them off of her face. Many of the sick babies had terrible diarrhea and there was no way to breathe fresh air. Cloth diapers were in short supply and plastic grocery sacks served as diapers. You can imagine the smell. It took your breath away minute by minute.

God used what seemed like the most depressing place to completely fill my heart. He let me find Him there. I knew I could love Sharon like a momma. What was I even saying? She needed a momma in that moment. Her time would be short lived on earth and I could do that for her. It was consuming. Weeks passed but in what felt like a second my time ran out. I had to get on a bus to cross the border into Kenya. I thought my heart would break wide open. God planted a seed deep within me for Baby Sharon. I never forgot her. Even as I moved to other countries and had life altering moments, Sharon was always on my mind.

Three months passed, and I was finally back home in the states. I had tried to email Eric and tell him about this sick baby who changed my life, but there was really no way for him to understand what happened in that damp room in the middle of Africa. I really struggled with my American life. Air conditioning made me uncomfortable and I struggled with radical guilt for all we had. I could not get anyone to understand. I now know why all these years later. I needed to walk through that pain alone. I needed so desperately to be changed.

Initially, my American mind thought I would get back to the states and figure out how to adopt Baby Sharon. I knew it would likely not happen and it wouldn't be fair to Eric to expect him to be ready for a family. We had not even wanted kids up to this point. I tried to keep in touch with the orphanage owner when I returned to the states. I was in contact a few times, and then nothing. I would email with no response. I learned much later that the woman who was running the orphanage had died unexpectedly. I never knew what happened to Sharon. There was no closure. Maybe that was not such a bad thing. Here I am, years later, and her portrait still hangs in my home, and forever in my heart.

God used Baby Sharon to show me my future. I knew from that point on, we would adopt. I knew it was not the right timing but one day when we decided to start a family, adoption was going to be our path. If I only knew then what I know now. That sick, beautiful baby changed so many lives. Fast forward to today, and we have adopted five wonderful little warriors and fostered so many more. God used Sharon in a radical way. What a painfully beautiful gift.

What has God used in your life that was beautiful and hard and messy? Maybe you are thinking...*nothing*. Maybe you are in the middle of your pain. Maybe you are coming out of a difficult season or you just feel kind of lost. All of these places can totally be used by God. He can fill our voids and give us a passion and mission we could have never imagined. All of it can come out of a season of pain. There is more, I promise.

Never in a thousand years would I have imagined that this would be my future. So, once again, God used my selfish ambition, patiently loved on me, then blew the doors off my life. We underestimate our pain and the good it brings. It is so difficult in the middle of sadness and grief to see the bigger picture. God can use all things. It doesn't mean some things are not horrible and unbearable, but He can use our pain to help heal others.

So, if you happen to be reading this and feel like you have really screwed up in life, have hope, my friend. God is a God of forgiveness and second chances. He will not walk out when life gets hard like some humans might. He is steadfast and true. He calls us to be strong. I want to be strong. Usually, it is in my own strength, but He almost always calls me to things I could never handle on my own. In our weaknesses, He is strong.

"Be strong and courageous. Do not be afraid or terrified because of them, for the Lord your God goes with you; He will never leave or forsake you" (NIV, Message Bible App, Deut. 31:6). [1]

Enough said. What is God calling you to?

CHAPTER 3
MILLION DOLLAR BABY

Adoption for Beginners

My not so tidy truth from Thailand to Africa, back to the real world and my ka-blammo into the momhood.

Once I landed and regrouped from my time in Africa, it was time to get a big girl job. Soon enough, I stuffed the emotions and life change that happened in Africa into a fancy designer bag and got to work. I was really good at work. I found my value in working hard. I started a sales job in the corporate world, and I felt happy to work, even if I was unfulfilled. It was a confusing time trying to process all I had been through in Africa. There was so much to process. I decided to go all in with this new job. I was not exactly saving the world, but I knew I could work hard and achieve.

Soon enough, it became my life. I set goals and blasted through them. I doubled my salary in commissions the first year. (I was such a big deal, in my own mind mostly.) During the next two years, I did the same and much more. I had never made much money in the past, but a six-figure income was fun. I filled my world with buying things to fill the giant gaping hole in my heart. My career took over and within a few years, my high ambitions had me running on fumes. I was traveling every other week from Missouri to Houston and Dallas. I rarely saw Eric. By then he was running a practice and we knew our lifestyle was not sustainable.

I finally decided to let go of the job that seemed to define me. Now, there is much more to that story but *Imma just give you the Cliff's Notes*. Eric had to man up, and I was about to "woman down". I was tired of being the main bread winner and I was out of fuel for the unfulfilling corporate world. I basically came home one random week after working in Dallas and told Eric I wanted to quit my job. He was kind of squirmy because he knew that meant he had to seriously step up his earning game. He agreed it was time for a change, said something along the lines of "Okay, let's decide on like 3 or 4 months and then you give your notice."

Then I followed up his comment with something exactly like, "I already gave my notice."

Mic drop.

I am kind of a loaded gun, all or nothing. I realize that it is not exactly a good quality. So, you can imagine what a good and solid whammo that had on my marriage. So basically, my marriage was on *Eeek*...not to be confused by fleek. The cash cow was leaving the pasture. Now we had to adapt. And by that, I mean Eric had to adapt, and pull up his big boy—with all the fancy schoolin'— doctor pants and get his game face on. Good bye, six-figure income for me. I guess I kind of peaced out.

Disclaimer: *Friends, I DO NOT RECOMMEND these actions. They are not smart or healthy or fun to live with.*

Feeling Nekkid

I felt naked, except not pronounced the normal way so much, but more southern...like *nekk-id*. That's more my style and closer to how I felt. (*I need to say right here that I fully embrace my hillbilly ways and words so please try to accommodate me if you are an upper class, well-mannered proper gal.*)

> All of a sudden, I had no income to show how important I was. I had nothing to tell me that I was enough. Not one thing was telling me I was good enough or happy enough or any of the one thousand things that seemed to lurk around my mind when trying to find even a tiny sliver of peace.

So there we were at a new place in life. You guys, I don't have a mind that rests easily. I am a natural born *doer*. So, uh-course, I had to move on to my next gig with barely a breath in between. I was ready to become a mom. Wait...that should read more like a question. Iwas ready to become a mom??? Wow. Talk about a pivotal time in a girl's life. I was 33 years old and for several years of marital bliss, we had no desire to expand this thing we called a family. Making the decision to be parents was kind of colossal. We knew in our minds if we were to ever have kids, it would be through adoption. Africa taught me that. But, talking about adoption and actually doing it? That's a totally different thang... and I do mean *thang*.

I don't really remember how it all shook out but getting to the "yes" took a second. I mean, it was fun to talk about and explore, but taking action was scary. I think Eric was kind of unsure, but he trusted me. And he knew I trusted God, so there we went. Full disclosure here: it was not nearly as tidy as I seem to be writing about it, but some details need to remain buried deeply.

Jumping Off the High Dive with No Floaties

Adoption game face on. Finding an adoption agency was weird. There was all this pressure, mainly that I put on myself. Once the agency was chosen, holy paperwork buried us. Dear Lord, it was a ton of paperwork. Home studies? Yikes. If you want to have someone get all up in your personal business, finances, marriage, and life in general, please run quickly to sign up for a home study. I was constantly thinking I was saying all the wrong things. Man, I was insecure, 'cause my fancy job was a thing of the past. Now, I was a stay at home wife, I guess, waiting for my infant child. What a bad title, I remember thinking. I cringed when someone asked me what I did. I wanted to tell them I USED to be a VERY big deal...but, that sounded pathetic. *Stay At home Wife* felt even more exposing. (Insecure much?)

A Note to All Mommas Who Are Birthing Babies

I have never given birth, so I am out of that loop. Though I just want to say right here, I think women do not get nearly enough credit for this child birthing situation. You guys are no joke, like the toughest women I know. I want to give you like a really fierce high five right now and throw you a party with Beyonce performing. All newly birthed baby mommas should get a rad party. Seriously. Well, if I was the President, it would be a thing, though Bae would get very tired of performing at each of your birth situations. Dang. I mean, please people! Lady birthers are boss. Period. End of story.

I knew exactly zero about adopting prior to jumping in. I had no idea exactly how out of control it all would come to feel in a very swift manner. I have issues, you see. I know that is hard to believe, right? This was 2007, so think how much more messed up I was then than I am now. You know, because now I am clearly sorted, up on my counseling game, and maybe just OK-er in my own skin.

Guatemala, Baby!

So, we delve into an international adoption from Guatemala. Days, weeks, months go by, filled with the infamous home studies both local and international, the security clearances, the approvals of so many places and things. You have to so carefully complete paperwork and notarize your face off. It was a daily routine that got very old, but I had my eye on the prize. I guess it was six months of this process before we were finally approved and added to a long wait list for our baby girl. I think we started at number thirteen on the wait list at that time. We waited and waited and celebrated every time we saw a family ahead of us get matched to their child.

Finally, the day came when they called to tell us they had a "referral" for us. This is when a child has become available and up for adoption. They sent over some minimal info, and two pictures. From there we would decide if this was our match. It was a really wild time with so much anticipation and excitement. I had played this scenario over in my head one thousand times. I remember feeling like I had waited my whole life for that email to come through. Finally, the day arrived. I called Eric and he was home in a flash so we could open the email together. I guess I thought the heavens just might open and bluebirds would perch on my shoulder singing a new song upon seeing our daughter for the first time.

As we sat together on the couch, the old-school, eerily-slow dial up internet loaded her pictures. We sat there silently, looking for such a long time. I think I was looking for that immediate, "Oh my gosh, that's my daughter" moment. Yes! Hmm… I wasn't sure how to feel. I mean, I couldn't tell much about her. She was a newborn. Newborns were not my jam. I was never the girl who wanted to hold someone's tiny baby. I never thought infants were particularly cute, except yours, of course. I knew zilch about babies. The pictures were not exactly taken with great care but more so snapped quickly and processed. I mean, didn't they realize we would be seeing our kid for the first time and I wanted to see everything, maybe with some heavenly music playing in the background? This was grassroots, friends.

I was just trying to see if she had all the needed parts. I was such an odd duck right at that moment. So, there we were looking at our kid. Geez. Just those words…*our kid*. So, what do we do now? We awkwardly agreed that this was our girl. It was kind of a clumsy exchange and then we just kind of did all the paperwork still trying to get it to sink in.

We were parents. I was a mom. I was still the exact same, wearing the exact same outfit I had been wearing 30 minutes before I became a mom...but now I was a mom. I became a mom at the loss of another mom. Dang. That was hard. I found myself thinking about the birth mom. A lot. So, while we were excited and thankful that God would give us a daughter, I did not take lightly the fact that it was at the total loss of another. So, as my heartache grew for the tiny girl in the photo so did my heartbreak for her birth momma.

It Is About to Get Real

To help with my heart-confusion, I bought a lot of stuff. I bought all the stuff you can imagine. The latest and greatest baby stuff. I continued to throw it all into that gaping hole.

I am sure none of you can relate to that, but I will tell you it worked. It worked, for about thirty seconds, and then I had to get back on the internet to look for more stuff.

It was fun to let everyone who had been following our story know that we had a daughter! We had so much wonderful support. Our families were blown away, happy and supportive. Just a few days after getting the photos of the baby, we were talking to Eric's mom. In passing, she mentioned that we should try to go see her over Thanksgiving, which was like a week away at the time. Would they let us do something like that? Is that even an option? After much pushing and prodding, we were sitting in an airport on Thanksgiving Day. The two of us were taking on the world, eating day-old airport pizza for a Thanksgiving meal, headed to meet our kid. I had so much stuff with me...many things so completely unnecessary to take care of a tiny human. At least I hoped it was enough things. I had no clue. I was happy and sad and excited and scared to death. We were really doing this.

I will never forget waking up the next day in Guatemala. We were to meet our kid face to face for the first time. Somehow, we had talked them into allowing her to stay with us at the hotel for the few days we would be there. At first, they agreed to daytime visits. Then the foster family would pick her back up every evening, but I pushed. I have no idea why I pushed so hard. Me and a tiny infant, whew. If I could only put into words how I felt that day. What a leap from the girl who babysat exactly four times growing up.

We had opted to really get a feel for the culture and went against the strong recommendation of our adoption agency to stay at a major hotel chain in the city. The tiny boutique hotel offered such an organic experience which I loved except for the fact they had no heat. Girl, wouldn't you know the few days we were there were the coldest they had experienced in years. Quickly my need to be authentic and all culture-y was out the door. There was no way we could keep a newborn in our freezing iceberg of a room. So, as we packed up our ten thousand baby products, our interpreter and foster momma were arriving. We had been on the lookout all morning for them. It felt like days as we waited for them to show up.

So, Now We Have a Kid

Finally, two women walked in with what seemed like twelve bundled up blankets. They were our people. My heart felt as if it would jump out of my chest and I needed to hit the toilets all at the same time. Sorry for the graphics, but to get a true feel for the experience, you gotta know that it was kind of a fight or flight deal.

We said our holas and slowly but surely, she started to unwrap the many layers covering the baby. I was guessing our baby could breathe under all that covering? When she finally emerged, she looked nothing like I had imagined from the grainy pictures. Her skin was so white, and she was covered in short black hair. Holy Lord in Heaven, this was my kid? I was like a whole other level as an official mom. What in the world?

The next bit of time was surreal. We decided to go with the foster family over to the new hotel. She sat up front holding the baby and we got in the back. I could see the ground move in the holes underneath our feet in the floorboard of the car. There we were in the car with total strangers who were caregiving for our baby, who was actually another woman's baby. They were sitting in the front seat holding her with no seatbelt or safety device. The circle never seemed to end. I was overwhelmed with emotion. I could not get myself together. Once we reached the hotel, I could tell the foster momma knew I had no clue what I was doing. I think she was scared to leave this tiny newborn with...of all people...me.

We finally got checked in to the Westin Camino Real. All of a sudden, all the wonderful grassroots tradition and simplicity of the culture was out the door, and we were back to high standard hotel living. All of the employees made it wonderful though. I was in my own zone, part bliss, part what the heck have I done? We went to the room and unpacked the many blankets covering the tiny one, and we looked at every square inch of her. We just stared at her for the longest time. She didn't do much. She pretty much just laid there. As an overthinker, I started to overanalyze my bonding with her. Did I feel warm and fuzzy? Did she seem to have a connection with me? She seemed to like Eric better…Ugh. Is this what I am in for the rest of my life?

He is always good at all the stuff. He keeps his stuff in perfect order. You can eat off the floor board of his car. Now he gets the kid, too? Of course, he does. Of course, she will love him the most. He has his shiz together. I am just a hippie, camouflaged as a modern mom. I am a flimsy extra in this family of three. The plus one. He even knew how to hold her better than me. Damn you, man! Why did I have to marry up so much?

My thoughts ran away with me. Time to hit the buffet downstairs. I needed to stress eat since I was not able to shop. We ventured out with the overly priced baby stroller in tow. Weird. As I sat and quickly ordered my Coca-Cola Light, I began to notice the people all around us. They were adoptive families just like us. Some of the women had the same look in their eyes as I did. I felt like I just exhaled after holding my breath for two hours. Our eyes met with emotion and terror. Okay, I am guessing theirs was not terror, but maybe a certain level of fear I could certainly connect with. We were all sorting out this new situation. I remember our adoption agency gently suggesting we should stay at this hotel. It was set up for families in the adoption process. And like always, committed to being unique and doing my own thing, we had taken another path to get to this place.

For Anyone Who Has Ever Felt Like a Total Failure...PLEASE READ ON.

For the rest of my life, I will never forget that first night we spent with Bianca. I had been edgy all day. I changed her outfit ten times. I tried to figure out what I needed to tell her since I knew we would be leaving her in such a short time. It was early evening and I was exhausted, but not because she was a difficult baby. She was quite the opposite actually. By 10 p.m. she was still up and wide-eyed. Eric and I were both so tired. Taking care of a baby is tiring y'all.

At that point, I was sure she hated me. I know how whacked out that sounds, but my thoughts were in such a strange place. People don't talk about the true crazy that happens in their mind nearly enough. She was clearly tired. She had hardly slept all day. And while I was no expert on newborns, I had heard they sleep a lot. Everything was new, and all the smells were different. There I was putting all of my freshly washed stuff from home on her. Nothing felt at all familiar to her. I am sure she was freaking out in her tiny body. Hey, I was freaking out too. So, I guess we had that in common.

Dramatic Much?

She started to cry and continued to cry unless Eric would hold her. Yes, Eric. You guys, by midnight (I am not even kidding in the least when I say) I was on my knees begging God for help. I had made the biggest mistake of our lives. I could not even take care of her. I was so beside myself. It's hilarious thinking back now. I had been the one who spearheaded this whole deal and now I could not even handle it. I was such a failure at parenting. I had to rest. Eric walked around the hotel with her until the early morning hours. I woke up in a panic when I did not see them in the room. I found them soon after in the hotel lobby asleep on a couch with another dad just one couch away with his baby. I fell in love, mainly with Eric. What a guy. He totally took one for the team. Maybe marrying up was worth it.

I left Guatemala a few days later wondering about my huge mistake. I am really trying to be honest in these words and even now, it's not written easily. Bianca never did really take to me on that trip. Maybe I took our basically perfect life and totally screwed it up. I cried on the plane most of the way home, but not for the reasons the other adoptive mommas were likely crying. I did not have a bond. I felt horrible about it. What was wrong with me? Maybe I was not cut out to be a parent. Maybe I had inherited some genetics that made me run from parenthood.

I remember everyone bombarding me with questions when I got home, and I lied. Over and over, I lied. I could not even remember the good stuff from that first trip because I was so overwhelmed by the fact that I ruined all of our lives. I am not dramatic at all, friends, just a consistent smooth sailor, as you can see.

What God Can Do With Our Crazy

One week or so went by and my heart started to ache. I had prayed over and over and begged God for answers. I was on my face in the middle of my perfectly designed nursery when God met me right where I was. I laid out in the floor for what seemed like all day. I prayed. I negotiated. I begged.

He met me and hugged it out in His Jesus-y way. He took my life right there in that room and filled it up. He released me from the years of pain I had held so heavy in my heart. When I was a kid, my bio dad chose another life. I never got over it. I never felt like enough. I was always trying to outdo everyone and everything to prove how great I was. The truth is (and was), I was just fine. I was just busted up a little bit from a lot of things and because of this, I felt like I always needed to prove myself. So far, I had sucked at parenting.

I was afraid. What if I woke up one day and decided parenting was not for me? Would I leave it all and run? I knew that I wanted to when we were in Guatemala. I thought I was not enough for this precious baby.

God met me on that hardwood floor that day and allowed me to cry until I could not cry even one more tear. Then He filled me with a passion and mission for this baby girl. I knew she was my daughter. I was enough. I could totally do this. I would screw up because that is one thing I rock at, but I would also love the crap out of her. I would raise her up to be a total dominator in all things life-related. I could do this. God could do this. (Wow, I guess that was a little foreshadow…because even at the ripe age of twelve, she be fierce!)

I got up off that floor on a new mission. I was wounded and totally bruised, and that was fine. I didn't get all fixed up that day where I would never have another daddy issue, but I got a bit of healing. Maybe sometimes that is exactly what we need, friends. A little bit of healing goes a long way.

Game Face

The next few months I held so strong. After making the trip to Guatemala, I realized it was not all that far to travel. I decided I would need to go frequently to bond with my girl. As you can imagine, one trip turned into several. It is a strange thing with international adoptions. You wait every day for a phone call. Every tiny step forward is such a win for the team. My control issues were on full bling as I tried to get the system to cooperate with the timeline that I had in my head to bring Bianca home. If we could just get her home by six months, life would be sweet. I could totally wait six months…barely. If I paced myself just right, I could make it. I had read story after story of people's journeys and some of them were not good. I was master-of-all-things-adoption-blog-worthy by that time. I followed everyone's everything adoption related and had created my own blog for people to find the latest updates on our adoption…mainly so they would ask me less.

(Side note: If you love someone in the adoption process—or if you breathe—we need you to know this: Please never tell an adoptive parent how long it seems like they have waited, 'cause they TOTALLY know. Never ask why it is taking so long.)

Get This Kid Home Already

By my third trip to visit Bianca, I knew most every employee in the hotel by name. The Westin Camino Real had become my second home. I would only go about three weeks without seeing her and then I was hopping back on a plane. I usually rolled in midweek and Eric would fly in for the weekend. I know, what a brat. Turns out quitting my job was awesome. Sometimes I took my mom and other times I went solo. It was a surreal version of life being lived in that hotel. We would just look at each other, me and B. Then most days we would head down to the pool for a little sun and chill. That was the life.

I think I was just a handful of trips in when I met a woman. I was so intrigued by her. She almost seemed like she lived there. I could see her each visit with her Guatemalan daughter. Her baby was about 18-months-old. One day we connected poolside. She began to tell me her story and my heart sank. She talked about their journey. They had so many complications. She had three other kids in the states but eventually had to move to Guatemala to fight for her daughter. They had been living in the hotel for over six months. I was devastated for them, and us. I knew very well her story could become mine. I learned just how little control I had over the whole adoption process and it was mind boggling. My eyes had been officially opened to the process and I did not like it. There was a lot changing with adoption in Guatemala and the prognosis was not good.

My six-month goal came and passed with little to no movement. By now, my heart could burst for my daughter. I was a good mom. I could actually do this mom gig. I spent many days back in the states on the floor in her nursery; the same spot I found myself months earlier but for a very different reason. I tried my best to negotiate with God. If He would just bring her home, I would do ALL the things. My pleas fell short as I knew God was calling me to release control. It was all an illusion anyway. My trips increased.

I was seeing Bianca every two weeks instead of three. Once I was in country, I would spend a week with her each time.

This is where her nickname "Million Dollar Baby" comes into play. It was funny, and a little too true. It was right around the time the movie with the same name came out. I would not budge on my travel plans and Eric was not about to tell me no. We got one set of bad news after another for a while. Our case would go to court only to find something was not signed or initialed or some other totally ludicrous thing. Weeks became months and there she was, 10-months-old in Guatemala waiting for us.

We had so many people who followed our story. I had arrived at a place where I just could not handle going out in public. People had the very best intentions, but I could barely handle the fact she was not home and the last thing I wanted to do was explain to someone else why it was taking so long.

Then one day, it finally happened. We got the call. I will never forget that day. Everything had finally cleared in court and they were setting her embassy appointment. This meant she was coming home. I was beyond bliss about everything. Our town rallied when they heard the news.

The good news spread fast and we were quickly on a plane for our final trip. By this time, we cherished the people who worked at the hotel and the friends we made there. It was hard to see my friend there every month, without change. Even as we were on our final leg, their progress had stopped completely. What a heartache. I always work through in my mind why things have to happen the way they do, but I have very few answers.

One of the sweetest days in my life was the day we stepped off the plane back in the USA with grands and friends waiting eagerly to see this little wonder. She was worth every second of the pain and sadness, the hoping and praying. So, if you are reading this and adoption has not been in your path, I know you can likely still relate. We all have things we've longed for, hoped for more, and asked God for. God has such a unique way to teach us. That was my first true taste of how much God loves us. The love I felt for my daughter blew my mind. I wanted the world for her. I wanted to protect her and nurture her and never let her go. Imagine how much more God loves us. It is kind of mind blowing.

We can't always get handed our heart's desires. I never could have learned the lessons I did if it had all come easily to me. We tend to want to get out of painful situations. Most times something much bigger than we can imagine is happening during those long waits.

> I still struggle with sitting patiently in the trials. I think it is our human nature to want to fix things. I am a fixer, but sometimes things are not meant to be fixed, but instead lived out.

My fave boss pastor, Steven Furtick, said in a sermon, "The challenge in front of you is indicative of the power within you."

No truer words.

Y'all, just like that, she was my size.
Wearing my stuff. Taking my things.

Busting selfies on my phone every two seconds

CHAPTER 4
THAT INSTA FILTER AIN'T REAL LIFE

Looked easy enough…See? That's what happens in pictures.

Do you ever look at pictures of families on social media and think, if only? Me too. I had that life in the picture once. Well, I didn't *truly* have the life in the picture, but it felt pretty damn close. We had a business that was booming. We were spending right along with it. We had adopted our daughter, Bianca, from Guatemala and right after we got her home, God told me were supposed to adopt from Africa! So, fast forward two years, and we also had

Solie from Ethiopia. We had the two kids and the Land Rover to complete my shallow image of bliss and goals.

My kids were dressed delightfully most times, and I did not look bad myself. You guys, my face looked so young back then. No chemicals pumped in back in those days, just straight up youth. I would get frustrated and tired at the most random things because that was my life of privilege. If someone decided to ask us to lunch and it was during kid nap time, forget about it! I had to keep my girls' nap time on schedule, and it was bonkers to even think about us getting off track. Come on people, have a little common courtesy! Ha.

This all sounds kind of funny to write about since I am just about the least structured person in America. I think back then because I was so radically insecure at "momming," I tried to live by lots of random rules when it came to my girls. I started out organic, too. I boiled bottles and we went for leisurely trips to Target multiple times a week. I had matching car seats. I am saying, life presented sweetly on the surface even if it was coming to a boil underneath.

Big Pimping in Small Town 'Merica.

That was my #currentstatus back then.

I never missed a day at the gym after a leisurely morning with the girls. They went to a lovely little child care there (which is one of the best ideas in all of creation, by the way). I could pump the iron or suck down a snazzy coffee drink and get a break from my severely stressful life. Ha. That was a time of life when I had no clue how sweet I had it. But that seemed to be life in general. It is like when you pray and ask God for faith. "Dear God, I just want to trust you so much more." Oh, sweet sister, hold on to your everything, 'cause when He answers that prayer, prepare for total annihilation of your current life.

> To have more faith, we actually have to live through stuff where we have no control of the outcome. Only God.

Eric was working his butt off and bringing home the cheddar. The more he made, the more we seemed to spend. No saving for this family! I had no idea how stressful his life had become. He pretty much had to figure it out, at lightning speed when his sugar momma quit corporate America four years prior, just because I felt like it. I had to give him some serious street cred on that one. Here we were a handful of years later in a whole new phase of life.

I noticed as his client base grew, so did his long hours at work and also his stress level. Sure, we had the cars and the stuff, but I could feel him starting to slip just a bit. Over time, I would catch him with the most intense (not in a good way) look on his face. He would slip into this mode when something did not seem to go his way, or for maybe no reason at all. I would catch him sitting in the living room on the weekends staring out into dead space. He would totally check out. He was starting to have a quicker temper and he seemed less and less like himself. He had always been a Type A personality, but this was taking it to a new level. Slowly, it seemed that joy had left the building.

Our kids were pretty easy back then and even though parenting was new, there was not a lot of stress happening as a result of the girls. So, although they added to the mix, kids were not the reason for the radical change. Months went by and the noose seemed to tighten. We would fight. Oh man, would we fight. I started to dread him coming home at night. I remember thinking we better have an awesome time during the day because dad was coming home, and I never had a clue what kind of mood he would be in. I loved him so much, but I handled his stress in all the wrong ways back then. I let it consume me. I was terrified that our girls would grow up and be afraid of him. He was nothing to be afraid of by any means, but his intensity tended to shut the house party down fairly consistently.

I started to wonder if this was going to be our life. I didn't like this life. We were growing farther and farther apart. I am sure he felt alone and so did I. As Eric's mood began to spiral downward, I began to feel like a caged animal. I was the actual momma bear out to protect her cubs from his mood swings.

It was a barrier that I had no idea how to talk about…to anyone. Everyone thought our lives were so easy and sweet. I was young and had no real clue how to express myself when it came to the actual crappy hard stuff in life. Even my really good buddies did not seem to have anything like this happening in their worlds. On the outside, Eric had it all figured out. He was Mr. Positive for everyone. His days at work were filled with people's needs. He practiced chiropractic, but he might as well have been a psychiatrist. People came to him with everything. They knew he could encourage them and help them through their tough life situations. It was draining him. He loved to help people. His heart was then, and still is, so huge for the human spirit, but it was becoming too much.

I remember one night he was supposed to be home from work to lead a small group we held at our house each week. I was sweating it. I mean HE was the leader. I hated leading that stuff. You know when you are 'kind of' a leader, but you live with Dr. Phil? Yeah, okay, if you can relate to that, then you can relate to me. The time for the group to start had come and gone. Everyone was there, and I was stalker calling him every five minutes. Thirty minutes into the group time, he rolled in. I was so hot I could barely speak to him.

He came into the room and sat down and everyone kind of got quiet. Out of what felt like nowhere, he started to tear up. He went on to tell us that he almost didn't come home. He wanted to get in his car and start driving and just keep going as far as he could go. What? Uh, what was he even talking about? He went on to tell us about how it felt in his office. So many people needed him all the time. His staff would buzz him to come downstairs with a full house of patients and he felt paralyzed. He would have to pep talk himself into going down the stairs. He was functioning on autopilot. He was miserable. I had no idea. I felt awful that I had not been better support. At that time in my life, I could not relate to Eric at all. I had not felt those feelings of hopelessness. I could not imagine that he felt that way…ever. It was all a shock to my system. I wanted to help him but had no clue how to do it.

I remember the group coming around him that night and we all just prayed for healing. I think he felt a little freer just being honest about what he had been going through. Soon enough he was back to work life and I suppose I hoped he had been totally healed. I think it scared me so much at the time, I unintentionally decided to just avoid it altogether. You guys, my biggest fear was always him leaving us…dad baggage. So, to hear Eric say he wanted to get in the car and drive far, far away punched all of my fear buttons.

How NOT to Deal with Problems

I bet you can imagine how much ignoring our problems helped. Yes, girl, you are right. Things went from bad to worse. I felt like he was so fragile, I walked on eggshells around him to try my best not to upset him. This choice was lame on my part. Instead of talking to him when I was frustrated, I stuffed it. I did not want to make his life more stressful. Imagine living life like this when you are geared up to be a total truth teller. No matter how perfect I tried to make home life, of course it was never enough. He was dealing with a giant I could not slay.

Life went on and got much more intense. I got to the point I felt like I had to decide for me and the girls. We couldn't stay in this environment. Eric and I had a wonderful business mentor at the time. I showed up to meet with him and I spilled all the beans. I had been miserable. No one could win in our home. Nothing was ever enough. We were a mess. That day he had Eric come in to his office to meet with us. The next two hours were intense.

A Change is Coming, One Way or the Other

Our friend and business mentor was the only man who could speak so directly to Eric. Let me tell you about this guy. Have you ever had God drop someone in your life out of nowhere and stay for just a certain period of time? He was almost like an angel. We had met him about a year and half prior to this day. We had an idea for an invention. (It was pretty awesome, by the way.) Someone put us in contact with Steve, so we could get some feedback on our idea. We had really no idea what to do with it other than we knew it was solving a problem. After meeting with him and walking through some of the steps to see if our product was viable, we learned there was no solid option to get it to market.

Instead of parting ways, Steve dug in with us. There was no reason for someone in his position to stay connected to us. He was radically successful in business and just a wonderful human. We really needed someone exactly like him in our lives. He decided to work with us. He mentored me and we created a business together to help new inventors. He would serve as an angel investor as we worked on products. It was phenomenal. He taught me so much about business and how to actually accomplish goals instead of talk about them. He was hard on me at times and I loved it because I knew it was for a higher purpose.

Steve also took on coaching us with our current business. He helped Eric innovate our company and he pushed us to be better. Through this process, we grew to trust him like few others. Eric had not had a lot of solid men in his life to trust. So, I knew Steve was the only man who could have pushed Eric to make a change in his life. He had earned it. He was tough and that is exactly what we both needed in this situation. I knew he cared for us and wanted the best for us, but he would not tolerate us staying in an unacceptable living situation. God used him that day in such a radical way.

He finally told Eric that if he did not get help that day, I would take the kids and leave him. He was right. I could not even begin to imagine my life without Eric, but I knew what was happening at home was not sustainable. Eric could hardly believe we were giving him that ultimatum. Being a chiropractor to him meant taking no medicines for anything. Y'all, I told you my main man was extreme. He is the guy who has likely never taken an aspirin for pain of any sort…his whole life. So, in comparison, we are complete opposites in that area up until this point. I was the ibuprofen queen growing up. Here was someone Eric loved and trusted telling him if he did not get help, and likely on meds, he was going to lose his family.

That was a serious situation and major decision for Eric. We literally asked him to go against everything he believed in his own mind about taking medicine or risk losing his family. He felt like and had completely convinced himself that if he were to be diagnosed and take some sort of medication, he would have to stop being a chiropractor. He was so misled in his own mind and yet so certain of his reality. If I have ever been in a "Come to Jesus" kind of meeting, this was it. There was one point I thought he was going to let us go. I could see everything within him in agony while he considered his options. His belief system was being severely challenged. We cried and yelled some and talked and cried some more. I thought the breakthrough would not come and then finally in a moment, Eric exhaled and agreed to get help.

Red Sea Moments

Wow. I could hardly believe his words. The past few hours felt like days as we hashed it out in the boardroom of Steve's office. You mean to tell me there is hope? I could hardly believe my ears.

We had a family friend who was a psychiatrist. She was willing to see us that very day. She understood we were in a unique situation. Now, I am no stranger to counseling, friends. I have several thousands of dollars' worth of counseling feedback as I am sure you can imagine after reading my thoughts. But that day was different. I felt like she was holding a key that we had been searching for. It was years in the making that brought us to the breaking point. It was a very tender and vulnerable time. The heaviness of the chance of me leaving Eric made it hard to make eye contact.

As she started to ask Eric about his life and thoughts, it all began to unravel. We didn't know heading into it if he was bi-polar or depressed or what. She diagnosed him with severe anxiety. She compared the anxiety to a thread that is being wound tighter and tighter until it one day it would snap, and that day was very close. The little things that are normal stresses and come with having kids were a much bigger deal to him. He was feeling bombarded with all of the needs of others. He was fixing everyone except himself. It was so eye opening and it gave us such hope. I had been running very low on hope up to that point.

Our friend prescribed him a basic anxiety med and he filled it immediately. He continued counseling and started taking the meds and it felt like no time until I got my old Eric back. Now, I know that sentence sounds all rainbows, unicorns and glitter farts, but it kind of felt like that at the time. I had no idea how much pressure we had all been living under. I was at home every day raising two little girls while Eric was at the office. We were living two totally separate lives but under one roof. How could we be married and be so totally lost from each other? It was a charade we did not even know we were playing. It was not like we had just gotten married and we did not know each other. We totally knew each other, however, we had been slipping apart for a long time. It is wild how quickly my marriage went from sweet to salty.

The Sobering Truth

Life did not become perfect after Eric got on meds, but it changed. It changed us at our core. I looked at him differently and I know he did the same with me. For a long time after it all shook down, I was reminded daily of how different things could have played out. What if he would not have been willing to totally check his pride and get help? Even worse, what if he did get to the end of his rope? What if one day he just got in his swanky car and drove far away to never come back to us? It was possible. It is possible. Life is hard on marriages. The enemy wants to cause constant division. He uses our weaknesses. He preys on our fears. I hope you hear me, girls. It starts with small stuff and becomes an avalanche. If your marriage feels kind of in the tank, that is NO JOKE. The enemy wants to steal and destroy families.

I was scared back then for people to know how hard things were for us. Still to this day, I write very carefully about this particularly hard time in life out of respect for my marriage and family. What would they think of us? We were new parents, looking like life was going swimmingly, but we were actually barely sleeping together. I was going through the motions and dreading Eric's arrival home every night. Imagine how that must have felt for him. We wonder how affairs happen. We are judge-y when friends around us get divorced and make bad decisions. Why? Why do we do that? We were and are always are a handful of bad decisions away from something that would forever alter our lives; the game changing stuff that would rip our families apart. No one is immune to this and if it feels like you are, you better run, girl, run!

So, I am aware. All of the time. I'm not about to judge your marriage because I sure don't need you judging mine. No one knows what happens under another's roof. We think we know, but I assure you we don't. Things are not always as they seem. Pain stinks to go through. I would really prefer a life without it. It is the deep pain that shapes us though. Without enduring my pain, I cannot relate to you. I cannot share my story and set you free, set myself free. Maybe someone reading this will relate.

Maybe someone else is living with an awesome partner who has lost their way. Maybe you feel alone and hopeless and believe this is how it has to be. I want to scream out to you…TAKE YOUR LIFE BACK! Kick and fight and plead for a better marriage. You deserve it! You are worth it. If you have a partner who needs help, or you need help, reach out and ask for it. You are not alone. Couples struggle. We need freedom in this area to be authentic. It is helping no one when we carry on and act nice while our souls are withering away. We must fight for our best lives.

I hope you dig in and put your big toe in the ocean of freedom. I am just getting started but I would say I am about cankle-deep in it and it feels right nice. I have the battle scars. I might as well share them with the world.

CHAPTER 5

THE CHAPTER I ALMOST DELETED — HEAVY DRINKING AND SLOWLY SINKING

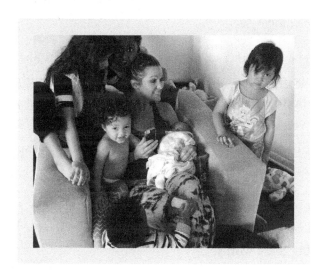

Like a Bad Country Song, But My Real Life

Here I am. I feel like I am standing stark naked in front of you. Ok, maybe not totally naked, but definitely awkward on a level fairly close to that. Maybe I should paint a better picture to portray my feelings. Won't you join me in this word picture? So, let's say as a grown woman in my 40's, I went to a required somehow pool party and I showed up without a suit. The next thing I know, someone offers to let me wear one of their extra suits, which gives me anxiety just thinking about.

Let's say I must accept this offer to wear the bonus suit of my acquaintance. I go to put it on only to find it is embarrassingly ill-fitting and I am by no means prepared (if you know what I mean) for swimsuit season…not to mention the suit is several sizes too small in the tush and boob regions. I have absolutely no choice in this pretend scenario and everyone is waiting for me to emerge. As I trip and fall on my way out of the dressing room, there you all are in full shock and awe. I know you can never unsee this. You're welcome.

I want to be brave and actually finish this chapter. I know it might help someone even though I have literally avoided finishing it for months. So, here goes. Ever feel like you have been fully exposed in a way you can never turn back or get a do over? This story feels like that. I know writing these words will open a new space to be judged and that, for me, is scary.

Here is just another place life went rogue for me. I'm not sure when it started exactly, this level of unraveling, but I'm feeling heart sick just writing these words.

I was lost. It was one of the many times in my life I felt invisible. Have you ever felt that way? Like maybe truly no one sees you? It is a lonely place we tend to go to and if we aren't careful, we stay there and sit alone. It is dangerous, friends.

It was a time I had trusted my gut and kind of hung on for dear life. I'm not even completely clear how it came about. I had always been a huge advocate for people in need, likely the reason I became an adoptive mom. When I heard sporadically about foster care, I just knew it was something I was not cut out for. No, thank you very much. I mean I was just a few years out of my marriage crossroad. It was like one major thing after another with very little breathing room.

One random night out over dinner and drinks with friends, as you might imagine, a major conversation came up about the need in our area for foster parents. It is hard to unknow things once you are aware. Learning about the desperate needs in our own community was sobering. After that night's conversation, the gate had officially been opened. See, I am an enneagram #8- The Challenger. I am a born justice seeker. The whole 'can't un-see what I have seen' is no joke in my world.

It was only a matter of time before fostering would enter my life. I will say it was led more by my husband than myself. After lots of talks about the need locally, Eric said something so insightful which I downplayed as lame at the time. "What if the right kid comes our way but we don't have our license to foster? Then we could never be a placement. We could never help make a difference."

Ok, so just do the classes. Baby steps, right? No commitment.

"Just Take the Classes", She Said

Foster care. These were two words I never thought would rule my world, but there I was. We signed up. We took the classes. Eight weeks. I wanted to leave every single week and never go back. It is a very honest course to prepare you for the real life that is about to be all up in your grill. Looking back, I am kind of thankful for the frankness. It helped, a little.

So, somehow there we were in what seemed like a flash. Our classes complete, and whammo! Our first foster placement. I was so sure in my newish foster parent brain that I could totally help make a difference. I was on a mission. I mean, I had been able to control most things in life. I could definitely make some much-needed changes in the system...or so I thought.

Well, classes finished and in one hot second, we had our first placement. Once we took our first placement, life seemed to take a turn I did not see coming. I was quickly overwhelmed and always seemed to be unprepared to handle the day to day life of a child's deep pain. It played out in so many ways that were foreign to me. Looking back, our previous adoptions were smooth compared to this. Now we were dealing with a history of abuse and exposure to things I could never understand. There was anger and pain and deep heartache for all involved.

It started out innocently enough. There was laughter and play amongst all the kids with a slow intro to the pain. "We can help! I know we can! We will not give up no matter what!" Because, only weak people give up. And I am NOT weak. (That is me, in case you wondered, but I am guessing you have a pretty good beat on me by now if you are still reading.)

Soon enough the anguish played out in significant behavior challenges. Massive acting out was happening in all kinds of ways and everyone was lost. I wish I could tell more of the details of our story but out of respect to all involved, I will keep our story just that, ours.

What I will share, which is the only part that is truly mine to share, is that I was drowning. In case you are thinking of ditching this read, please know: This is not a PSA on how fostering is bad!

Have you ever felt so good about something and then so bad? Have you felt like you have let all the world down around you? If you have, then maybe reading my failures will help you realize you are not alone.

A few months into our first foster placement, I was not functioning well (understatement of the year). I had no clue how to help our new kiddos (there were two now, by the way). In addition, I was starting to hate myself for ever choosing to do foster care. I had plenty of people who loved me tell me what a bad idea it was. To be clear, these are good people. They were fearful of the unknown because…aren't we all?

We had just adopted two daughters. Bianca had been home from Guatemala for a handful of years. Once we got home, it seemed like no time until God said, "Hey girl, let's do this…adopt from Africa" and after a very brief encounter over lunch with my awesome husband, we agreed to start the adoption process for Ethiopia to adopt our daughter, Solie.

You guys, God is no joke. He does not play. When we say we are ready to follow Him and trust Him, we had better be ready. I will never forget the exact day just a few years prior when God made it clear we were supposed to adopt from Africa. Eric came home one day for lunch innocently enough only for me to drop the new Ethiopia adoption bomb on him. I mean, we had just gotten the Million Dollar Baby home and settled, and here I was again saying it was time to jump back in.

Y'all, I have a rock star for a husband. I will say it *yet again and again*. I bet a lot of times he would have liked to tell me to shove it, but he never has. So, in no time we were plus two baby girls, a mom and dad and now foster care? Now add two additional kids to the mix. I think adding two children to any assortment of a family is a challenge. We were dealing with something on a much different level.

In the vein of honesty, here I will also say I am not exactly Susie Homemaker. I love my kids ridiculously. I also never want to babysit yours. I mean that in a gentle way but also, I'm serious. I never really babysat growing up except for a couple of families who let me go after a few babysitting disasters. I am not a big kid connector. I am a huge advocate for kids in need. I love to buy kid stuff which you could probably guess, but I am not naturally drawn to kids. If you have ever wondered if God has a sense of humor, the answer is emphatically, yes!

Goodbye, Fancy Me

I remember the day I had to trade in my fancy Land Rover for a giant Suburban. What the hell? It was like a bus. I felt like it was so long, you could throw a football in that thing. But to be clear, I would never even own a football to throw...so. Who drives these things anyway? Oh yeah, people with a ton of kids. I remember looking in the rearview mirror driving all four of the kids home one day thinking, *God, you really messed up this time.* I was coming out of my own skin right about then.

Foster care, and the pain it brought to my already damaged state, was royally kicking my butt. I started doing all the things to avoid my real life. In my heart, I knew our placement would not work. I knew it deep in my gut. I ran from it. I would never give up on a kid. I would never quit. I could never quit. I am not a quitter. That was hitting too close to home with my past.

> I swore I would never be that lady; the one who gave up when it got difficult. I would never be that woman who couldn't handle it.

I have some wonderful and powerful women in my life. Some have hung in through thick and thin and over time others have dropped off. That is life. Seasons happen. I am a lot to handle anyway. This particular season in life seemed to be one radical leap of faith after another, leaving the perimeter friends asking all kinds of honest yet prickly questions to each other...instead of me. (And I am not a "talk amongst yourself" about me kinda gal).

"Doesn't she realize she does not need to earn her way into heaven?" Ok, my church-y friends here.

"When is enough, enough?"

"Have you seen her? She is always out drinking with her girlfriends."

"I think she has a problem." (Boy, did I).

"We are worried about her. I mean we will never say anything directly to her, but we can talk about it amongst ourselves frequently." Wink. Wink.

Listen, I am throwing zero stones here. I have done the exact same thing. We do some really strange stuff as women. My true girlfriends knew I was struggling. Our backyard evening girl time hang outs started to increase, and I found my only source of retreat was in the wicker loveseat under the gazebo about three drinks in. I was slipping deeper and deeper. I had no idea how to live. I was living a lie for months. I was letting everyone I love down, and also trying to keep up the good lie to others that we were fine. I wasn't about to show my weakness. Honestly, back then, I'm not even sure I would acknowledge I had weakness.

My Sisters, We Are Missing the Real Stuff

I remember going to church during this time. People were so proud of us. Impressed even. It helped my pain a little, hearing their words of praise. Or maybe it stroked my pride if I am honest. Then I would lie to them and say things were fine and we were doing just great. What a great looking lie we lived. I'm sure people had to know the truth. They had to know I wasn't myself. Most people didn't ask too much.

> Foster care is an odd thing. Have a baby and the world throws a party. Become a foster parent and everyone gets awkward.

It wasn't too long until my partying (and by partying, I don't mean the 'having so much fun' kind) ways would catch up with me. It really was my escape at the time. I will never forget when someone from the church let me know that I would no longer be needed to sing on the worship team. Say what? Oh, right, "Susie" had complained about my unchristian behavior. I guess I was not exactly the best representor of the Big Man in those moments. You know what though? That was my real life happening and I was begging for someone to see me and I had zero skills to ask. I was sinking and just about to get carried out with the tide. I needed one of those crappy little inflatable doughnut floaty thingies thrown my way.

Sisters, we must see each other. We have to step up and look out for each other and speak truth in love. It was a lesson that would later move me to really see people in their current state and judge a whole lot less.

What I Know for Sure

Typically, people are not their actions. Actions are many times a result of the pain rolling through one's soul at the moment. Funny how life can change. In the midst of a life that did not work, I was being initiated to the day-to-day world of fostering. Social workers, investigators, doctors' appointments, therapy, CASA (Court Appointed Special Advocate) workers, no-show parent visits, children's division….so many people to try to please and prove you have it all together. Then there was the court system. Wow. For a woman who ran the show most of her life, I was completely stumped to have basically no voice in court when it came down to it.

You guys, I had watched a ton of Law and Order. I was sure I had a lot to say and do in this case. I thought I knew what was the "right" thing. Actually, I was sure I was the only one who had a clue what needed to happen. I spent hours upon hours losing my mind and my vocabulary on all the people involved. If I just got louder, surely, they would listen. Over and over, I was harshly reminded that I had zero control, which I desperately needed to keep up this all-consuming lie.

When You Can't Be Who the World Needs You to Be

I will never forget the day I bucked up and finally told Eric I couldn't handle it anymore. It wasn't like he was totally out of the loop. He is a total hands-on dad and husband. Life had changed so quickly for us we had kind of lost each other once again. It had taken such a toll on our marriage. Who am I kidding? *I* had taken such a toll on my marriage. It was me. It had nothing to do with these sweet souls who blew in like a hurricane on my sheltered life.

Here is yet another side note on Eric. He never quits anything for any reason. He is an over the top achiever in all things. He does extreme things all the time. Exhibit A: Right now, he is exploring subzero bathing techniques. Cold therapy. It is extreme. You guys, he is legit in all things legitable (and yes, I am making that a word).

Telling him I couldn't do this anymore was like the straw that broke the camel's back. I finally did it. I had to throw in the towel, and maybe a bottle of vodka or two. When the words came out, they were final. I had nothing left to give. I was to the point where I had to either come clean or I was a flight risk. The risk of getting in my car and getting the hell out of my life for a very long time… hmmm. That sounds familiar?

This was the first time I felt like I was on the verge of a nervous breakdown. So, while I was in the midst of having to pep talk myself just to roll over and put my two feet on the floor to get out of bed in the morning, now I had to go on to disappoint everyone possible in my life. So, here I am, a woman (we are already so relentlessly tough on ourselves) about to break every single person's heart. It is an unexplainable feeling to have to end a foster placement. There is nothing harder on a child. There is nothing harder on a family. Repeated foster placements take such a radical toll on kids who have already lived through so much.

I remember those days following my decision still with such grief. Ugh, you guys, I am super-duper just completely putting my heart on the line even sharing this now…I felt like everyone hated me. Maybe you are even having a thought like "how could she just give up?" I get it. The system can be ruthless. Once we had turned in our notice to end placement, we were dead to them. The six months we spent together were at an end. The months that followed were even tougher.

Girls, I am going to say this to hopefully help another out. We never know what another person is going through. I did not even want to leave my house for months. I remember seeing people at Target and dreading them asking about the kids. Soon enough, it would happen, and I had to tell them it didn't work out as I choked back hot tears. I wanted to run away as fast as I could, but I knew I had to woman up. I honestly cannot tell you how many people completely judged me. It was a high number…and those were just the people speaking directly to me…not including those who were speaking about me.

"What do you mean it didn't work out?"

"Did she go back to her family?"

"What happened?"

"Well, I would have totally taken her. She was adorable. Anyone would want her."

So, so many painful words were said.

The list went on. Please, please friends, never say these words to a foster parent. Most of the time intentions are so good and I get that, but in this situation, less is more. We are already crushed. We already feel horrible that it didn't work out. You can never imagine the heartache and disappointment we hold against ourselves, or maybe I should speak for myself on this one. Actually, this isn't just for failed foster placements. We should offer little questions or free advice and feedback to anyone going thru pain. Instead, we should love on them and pray for them...and LISTEN. Talk less.

No matter whose life we are taking a good strong look at, be it this situation or otherwise, words cut deep. Guess what? That lady you are having a tough time with, she might be screwing it up three kinds of ways. She might also be hanging on by a thread. We need more heart when it comes to looking at others. The woman who is having an affair. The girl who cuts you off in traffic. The mom who acts like her life is perfect. We are all just trying to get by, my people. I needed a world of forgiveness, but mostly, I needed permission to forgive myself.

The Part of the Story That is Even Harder to Tell

I feel like I can trust you guys, but even more than my trust, God is flat out pushing me to be vulnerable here as I rewrite this for the 1000th time. This the rest of the story about that time in my life. When we had to stop the placement, we kept one of the girls. One went, and one stayed. We were not capable of meeting the special needs of one. Because we petitioned to keep one of the girls, the guilt was almost worse. I realize even as I write these words, I am exposing myself to radical ridicule. Maybe it is from the foster care community. Maybe it is from outsiders looking in. I just knew it was not right. And with that being said, I also knew we made life even more painful for the child we did not keep in care. I still deal with that decision up to this day all these years later.

The child we did keep in placement was an infant. I had been so distracted trying to meet the other child's needs, I hardly considered the baby's special challenges. She was in a very tough place when we got her at four months. I had taken her to all the appointments and seen all the therapists. Things were not going well for her. Looking back, her story is likely part of the reason God made the move He did in our lives.

As I started coming out of the dark place I had been in for months, I began to realize this baby needed me to fight for her. Like really fight for her. (It took me right back to my time in Africa with Baby Sharon.) I had been so consumed with our prior life situation, I was not even contemplating her reality. Everyone was going through the motions. All of the boxes were being checked but nothing was happening. She simply was not thriving. I remember seeing her specialist one day who said she really had no idea what to expect for this child as she grew.

Hold on.

What? Back that train up. What did that even mean?

She had a very tough stay in the womb. Life on the outside had not been so great for her either. She was still on morphine at four months when we brought her home from the group foster home. She had gotten such a raw deal in her tiny life.

I sat in the doctor's office and bawled. I wanted to start using my very loud voice on all the people. It was no one's fault. They were actually just being honest with me. Her case was a tough one. It was a, "We will just have to see," kind of thing.

So I Put My Go-Girl Pants Back On

Let me just tell you what rises up in me with anything that revolves around injustice. (Enneagram #8) Girl, you talk about lighting a fire under my worn-out, black legging wearing butt. God opened my eyes to this radical need. To be honest, I had always feared having a child with special needs. I was afraid I could not do it.

There, I said it. If I knew then what I know now. It is crazy, the things we fear. All the many, many things. There I was. I had a child with special needs. No one knew what to expect. God has a way of bringing me face to face with a lot of my fears. I don't know about you, but it has taken me a lifetime to learn that fear is a liar. It seems I have to re-learn it over and over. Right about the time I seem to master it in one area, it pops up like a freaking whac-a-mole in another.

Eric and I began praying over her and for her life. Y'all, never ever underestimate the power of prayer. I had to walk away from the business I had recently started with our business mentor to take on all of the therapy she would need. I had to close a chapter I loved dearly to serve another.

Sacrifice.

We got a plan of attack. Any time I was in a doctor's office or with a therapist, I decided I would never allow anyone to talk about possible negative outcomes in front of this baby girl. I began to bond with her in a major way. I was her advocate. She needed me to do the next right thing, and then the next right thing. God had chosen me in that time to be her voice. And Lord knows I have a voice for better or worse. The next year was wrapped up in 7-10 appointments a week with therapy after therapy, outside all of the foster care stuff. She had the most loving therapists rooting her on. We fell in love with all of them. God used those people and our family to change that baby's life. She was a miracle.

Side Note on Miracles

Listen up, mommas and ladies. Believe in miracles, even if you are tired and heavy burdened. Get your people to pray and lift you up. Be brutally honest with just a few and count on them to be your strength when you are weak. We must do this for each other. I will believe for you if you need, but I am telling you, never give up on miracles.

The Fog Started to Lift

It was a slow process. Maybe I was healing as much as she was. Thinking back about it now, maybe that is exactly what was happening. We worked and cried and felt frustrated wondering what was going to happen. Was all of this even working? Then one day there was the slightest shift. It was kind of like her eyes seemed a little clearer. Like she was maybe, hopefully—help us, Lord Jesus—possibly, coming out of her fog just a teensy bit.

Her world seemed to be less murky. She started to respond. You guys, it was slow. I am not finding all the words for the crazy nuts emotions I am having just thinking through it.

In a matter of time, she sat alone with no one holding her up. Hear me, gals, this was colossal. She sat alone! She had fallen like a ton of bricks for so, so long. We lost it!

She struggled and fought and finally conquered a one-legged army crawl. We went wild.

She began to vocalize...the smallest sounds at first. Then it was like she literally found her voice.

Everyone was stunned.

She did it.

God did it.

God used her to change everyone around her and, most significantly, me.

He took me at my lowest point. He knew exactly what I needed and loved me in spite of myself. Anyone sensing an underlying theme here in this old bird's life? Have you felt some of the same things and seen God heal some major stuff in your life, only to go on and kind of dismiss the miracle? Yeah, me too.

I was fully invested. I needed a win. I was still totally exhausted, but He redeemed me every day. Sometimes we win and sometimes we learn.

Let me tell you about that little spitfire of a child. She is still with us all these years later. As I write this book, she is in big girl school. She has very minimal long-term effects from her tough start in life. She is rocking it at school. She is fiercely brilliant. She has this uncanny and cool connection with God that occasionally exposes itself verbally and I want to melt.

So, all of that pain, and the bad decisions I made on my end? God handled it.

I now realize I was just a part of the story for our other first foster daughter. God needed me to step up when I did to get her where she was supposed to go. I still think about her a lot. On days when the enemy is trying to stick it to me, I feel the heartache and failure of not being the right person. I am guessing that will never end. It is a weak spot for me.

As most of us are uncomfortably aware, the enemy loves to tell us lies about the places in our lives we have failed ourselves and others. He loves to take a sunny day, when we are just loving our basic everyday life, and tweak it with just a few reminders of our past failures. One thought leads to others if we are not on our A game. Soon enough, we are sad and depressed and feeling like we are not enough.

The enemy has this way with women in particular, in my experience. He plants seeds so early on in life of all the ways we are not enough; shame, guilt, lack of potential. His goal is to break us down one tiny lie at a time. These lies breed jealousy and anger and resentment until one day, we are not even sure if we believe in God, or maybe our spouse, friends, or family.

Truth Bomb in Love

I want to challenge you, girls. This one thing can change the world, so listen closely. We have sisters right around us who we love, and they are sinking into deep places. If you are feeling a nudge about someone, whatever it is…DO IT. Say it. Tell them you love them and are with them and for them. And just be there. Don't stop being there. Always do the thing in your gut. People are dying for us to see them.

What if we take it one step further? How about that chick that is so easy to judge? What if we tried another approach? I have heard it said many times, the things we don't like in someone else are often a reflection of something going on in us. Maybe. People need a damn break.

> Life is hard. We are all doing hard stuff every single day. You don't have to be a foster parent to be a world changer, or to have a valid reason for life being tough. Life is just tough, and also beautiful.

It is the total garbage that allows us to see the real beauty anyway. Otherwise, when it's all thin mint Girl Scout cookies and chocolate bars, we will never be able to appreciate the true good all around us. So, let's do it. Don't just think about it for a second. How about we each grab two girlfriends and agree we are going to be there *for each other*. So, then when we come together for our ever-loving favorite girl time, we get about stuff. Let's do less talking about what is going on in other's lives, and more *doing* for them.

It is fun. It breeds deep and solid sisterhood. It changes things. It becomes a mission really, and I have seen God honor it in crazy ways. We agree to hit the homeless shelter together and do whatever they need. I am the last cook in the land, but we have gone in and cleaned out the fridge, brought it home and cooked all the stuff that was losing shelf life. You can't believe how God will help a regular girl make a casserole that looks like I know what the heck I am doing.

Do you know a new mom, someone who has had surgery, or suffered a loss, or otherwise? Take her a dinner, or a Starbucks. I bet a sister could use the caffeine. Maybe it is a frazzled mom that could just use a break. And for goodness sakes, let's branch out, ladies. We need to be serving everyone…not just the girl who looks like us! The act of doing in love…all of it and any of it, changes stuff. One small act is actually a huge gift in the eyes of another. Not everyone will get it, but some will. And to me, that is world changer kind of stuff right there.

My little overcomer. She has grown since this photo, but dang…this was in the heart of it.

CHAPTER 6

MOMMING, BOOB JOBS, & THE THING I SWORE I WOULD NEVER DO

Now That I Have Your Attention

As a dear friend once bluntly told me, "*It is actually not about us.*"

What is that you say? That does not process well with this lady right here because all things are typically about me. Even when they are not, my ego will do a figure four leg lock on the situation and get that jazz switched back over to focusing on *this girl*.

Nice. I know. Don't you want to sign up right now to be my friend? I'm telling you, I will never forget the day a "lady" told me those super heavy and honest words in her blunt and matter of fact way concerning my issue with becoming a foster parent…it is not about you, or me, or us. You know what? I did not like her much in that moment. How dare she? She probably had no idea of my special capacity for love that no other human on the planet could possibly relate to.

I had adopted Bianca and then Solie. Boom. Done. International adoption times two. Done. I was no lightweight to stepping out in faith, okay? And as you can tell, I was also super humble right about then. Wink. Wink.

Boss Moms

I remember going to Wal-Mart with my girls when I only had the two. I was so stinking proud of them. I was also exhausted at this new mom thing. I look back now and cackle thinking of how "stressful" my life was. You know what though? Being a new mom is no joke. Some women make it truly look so easy. I have a few girls in my world that are boss moms. I can share more info later on the various categories for boss moms, because there are a few. I am talking about that special group of mommas I would love to have been in a different life. The girl who grew up wanting to have a family, wanting to be a mom. You can tell these moms. They have a special swagger about them. In my young momming years, I think I held a teensy grudge against them because I was not like them. But over the years, these moms have taught me so much.

Now, I do not fit in this particular boss mom category. I am more on the opposite end of having life flow smoothly. I still love the business out of my kids, but I don't necessarily have it going on in the organization and skills department.

If You Wouldn't Say it About a Boob Job...

Since I know you are skimming this chapter until the boob job stuff, here goes...I would find myself occasionally at Wal-Mart with my girls. I was always blown away by the "free" commentary and advice I would get on what I would suppose is our adoptive family situation. Now if you get confused, try substituting the word "boobs" in the place of kid(s) in each line of commentary:

Rando Stranger: "Are they your kids?"

Me: "Uh, yeah...I didn't exactly find them in the parking lot."

Rando Stranger: "I mean, Are they your *real* kids?'

(Be cool, girl. Be Cool. Don't go bananas right here in front of this fool.)

"Again...hello. They seem real to me."

"Could you not have kids of your own?"

A Few Thoughts on What NEVER to Ask:

- Never ask how much it costs and why it is so expensive—just don't.

- It is like asking a girl if she has had a boob job and, if so, what did it run her.

- Did she pay for one or get a discount on buying a pair? *Oh, sweet Lord Almighty, help us.*

- And blatant staring. All the blatant staring.

> Great Rule of Thumb: When in doubt, boob
> job filter it out. Because you HAVE TO LAUGHor
> else you will bawl your tear ducts completely
> dry or lose your beans on someone.

The Actual Story

You guys, I knew better than shopping at Wal-Mart. Target has always been my jam. Something was a funk at our Wally World. I will never forget the few times strangers would ask why I adopted kids from so far away when there are plenty of kids in our town that need help. Girls, it used to light me up. It was pride and other icky stuff that was running my spirit, but I would get so angry when people made ignorant comments. I always had a very quick response on the tip of my tongue that would take them to their knees, but most times I kept it to myself.

I was an insecure mom. I had very few adoptive momma friends. I felt like no one understood my plight. I was so very sorry for myself. I really had no idea what I was doing. So, imagine the day a lady I barely knew laid it to me straight on foster care. She was a foster mom. Maybe we had met in passing a time or two. Somehow on this day though, all the things changed.

Meet Dawn. Then stranger, now one of my peeps for life….and yes, the psychiatrist from earlier. ('Cause nobody said I have to write this book in chronological order.) We have differing memories I'm sure, on how our conversation went that particular day. I do remember talking adoption and our mutual love for it. Within a few minutes, we started talking foster care. At the time, I really did not know anything about foster care. If I am being totally legit, I guess I had some weird stereotype of what I thought a foster parent might look like in my head, and it did NOT look like Dawn.

She was hip and a little rogue. She said what she wanted and had lived a previous life as a full out hippie tree hugger. I am sure of it. The conversation heated up as I learned more about our local foster care situation. Our community was suffering. Kids were coming into care daily as a result of the drug problem in our shiny little town. What? Everything seemed fine in my neighborhood. I was living with a big fancy pair of rose-colored glasses over on Fountain Street. Even as she talked, I felt the wall trying to crumble around me, but still I persisted in my mind. Foster care was just not for this girl.

I remember telling her how I thought it was so great she was open to foster parenting, but that I could never do it.

"I mean, it would totally break my heart into a million pieces. I would just love the kids so much I could never give them back."

Her comeback set me on fire. "You should love them that much. It's actually not about you, but them."

Hold yo' phone, lady. There is no way I can put into words how much those words cut to my core. Okay, first of all, it is *always* about me. Have we met? Geez. *All* the things are about me.

I could feel a burst of hot sweat beginning to form from my under-pits. Who did she think she was?

Well crap.

I hated her.

I loved her.

I am sure I exited that convo as quickly as possible. That was like way, way too much pressure on this girl. If I guess correctly, I probably filled the next few days with online retail therapy, because let's face it, I love fashion and obviously, I love myself. There is no better reason to buy more things to fill the hole that seemed to swing wide open and swallow a girl whole some days.

It was just a handful of weeks after that conversation when Eric and I had a serious conversation about foster care again. I was still not on board, but it was keeping me up at night. Surprisingly, Eric took the lead on this one.

And Then We Jumped

Was God calling us to do this? Honestly, those days are kind of foggy for me. I would love to share in an elaborate testimony how God used his flock of seagulls, I mean angels, (not the hair band) to drop down out of the heavens and plant visions of little cherubs in my head, but I would be lying.

I would pep talk myself back to the foster care classes every week, like I mentioned before. They would tell us all the horrible scenarios that could happen upon taking a placement and follow those with visual assault videos from the 1960's. You guys. The acting. The everything. It was like I was being punked.

Did you know the actual goal of fostering is to see the kids reunited with bio parents?

Wow, now that was a shocker. I had a lot of my own very specific opinions back then on who should and should not go back to bio parents. I had plenty of judgement to dole out for most any situation. I contemplated how I was going to change this messed up system while also considering how I would quit the whole thing most days.

In Case You Have Ever Felt Like a Chump

One night, during our foster care classes, we had a chance to talk about our biggest fears. I was checked out, likely due to bad video footage and the looming thought of potentially doing this foster thing. When it was my turn, I will never forget blurting out my absolute truth with an eerie intensity. "I am terrified of head lice. I mean, I don't think I could handle it if we got a kid with head lice."

Whew, I finally said it. I felt like a free bird. Wow. It had been in my night terrors and now I had released it into the world. The caged bird just sang. Almost as soon as I said it and felt the rush of freedom, I was snapped back into reality. People's faces. Uh. I thought we were being honest here. Too much? What?

Guys, I have moments of depth and I can also be very vain and shallow, I suppose. I had been so checked out I had not realized people had been pouring their hearts out about actual real-life heartache kind of fears and then I go the head lice route? *Well played, jackass.*

Let me just say, I was 36 at the time and had lived my whole life terrified of head lice. So, it was a real legit fear for me, people. Did I look like a pompous chump saying that in the foster care class? Uh, little bit. Any who, live and learn, ladies. I got to learn so very much.

Just making head lice fashionable right about here.

The Dirty Truth of Getting in the Trenches

Nothing prepares you for the truth of foster care. You can read and prep and get every room just right and then you get that first placement and your world stops.

Imagine an innocent child scared to death. Usually, they have been taken out of a crisis situation and brought to a home of a total stranger. There is nothing familiar. Many times, they have no clothes of their own. They have no idea when they will see their parents again. It is tragic.

It has been eight years since we became foster parents. I will tell you, there is not one decision that has been more life-altering in my world than this one. It's kind of funny that I don't even really remember if I felt God leading it. I know now He was because I would have never made it through the training and most definitely through all of the lives that have come through our home.

We have had good placements and very difficult ones. I think about how different my life would have been if we would have passed on foster care because it was so hard. I most certainly would look at least ten years younger. That is no joke.

You guys, I am not trying to brag, but in the seasons since our dip in the foster care pool, I want to profess right here: We dominate head lice! I am officially the conqueror of my biggest buggy fear. I laugh in the face of the louse. It is an evil and shrill kind of laugh that makes my stomach roll just thinking about those critters. None the less, head lice, you are dead to me!

I am guessing your head is itching right about now. Sorry about that. Foster care has taught me so much that I could never have learned on my own. Fostering has played an integral role in taking me apart brick by brick. I was so sure I knew who the parents were behind the kids.

I was wrong.

We Think We Know...But

During an early placement, I remember being so angry with the kid's mom. I mean, how could she make the choices she was making? She was constantly letting everyone down, mainly her kid. Usually, I had to pay for it. Visit after visit, we would show up. Sometimes, on our end, we had to move heaven and earth to get there on time, with several of my other kids in tow. I was usually peeved because I knew she was not going to show up. But every single time, there sat her child, waiting hopefully.

We would arrive in time. We would sit. I would watch her child's face slowly drop as the minutes ticked away. I was so tired and ragged, I had a hard time seeing it for what it was. Maybe I wasn't as ragged as I want to say that I was. The reality was just too hard to swallow week in and week out. It was easier for me to be angry. I was angry. I was angry that I busted my butt to do all the things to get to a meeting that I knew would never happen. I was frustrated that I would actually be the one to pay for the fact that mom never showed. Her lack of action would play out in radical ways in my family life, in a child that had no skills in expressing her true sorrow. None of us knew how to express our sorrow.

Tuesdays. For so long, even after that child moved on, I despised Tuesdays. I never even realized it until I said it out loud to a friend one day. "Why in the world do you hate Tuesdays?" she would ask. I didn't know other than they felt dark and like it rained every single Tuesday. But, in fact, it was every single Tuesday for a time that our world was turned upside down and not out of mere inconvenience. Out of pain.

One child's pain can fill up a home. There was no making it better or smoothing it over. We just had to sit in it. Every week there was a new hope and every week a little face was crushed by a truth too painful to process.

Man, I couldn't stand that mom at the time. I had all the thoughts in my head and played out all kinds of real-life conversations I would have with her one day. I was going to tell her. I had big plans with all of my big words. I was going to totally set her straight.

I was clueless.

I had so much judgment in my heart and so little understanding. I used to go to court on behalf of my foster kiddos and I was always on fire. I made such a fool of myself on so many occasions when my own will got the best of me. Don't get me wrong, there were times when dealing with a few people when most anyone would lose their cool. But I was primarily operating from the world according to me. I don't know what it was that finally clicked for me. I really wish I knew how God worked all my crazy out. Okay, a little of my crazy.

> When I was able to see my kid's birth parents differently, stuff changed. Most parents in these circumstances come from tough situations. Most never had a life like I had the privilege of living. I only knew my experience, so I judged them based on that. I was wrong. Dead wrong.

Most of the sweeties I was fostering had parents who were also in and out of foster care as kids, and if not, sometimes their living options were even worse. How easy it was for me to look at them and think they should just get it together when many of them never had even the most basic examples of healthy love and structure in their own lives. Getting off drugs is not as easy as my judgmental soul believed.

Imagine growing up around abuse and unhealthy relationships with men. Nothing is safe, and nothing is sacred. Now add drugs to the mix. I'm cutting lots of corners here but trying to get to a quick point. Just because we think we know how things should be does not mean we understand the plight of another. And listen, you are preaching to the choir when your comeback is something along the lines of "It is still not fair." Nope. Definitely not fair. But we have to choose to live our lives with our eyes wide open. Blaming will get us exactly nowhere. Am I excusing the horrible situations these kids are coming from? Hell, no, but I do know we must be a part of the solution.

A Step of Faith Can Change Your Whole World

As a part of our fostering journey, we used to do what is called emergency placement. It is basically when a child or siblings come into care during the night and the team needs a day or more to find the right place for them. They would call us. My phone rang all hours of the night. I will say, this was my sweet spot. I never had a clue what I was walking into. I always knew there was a little person on the other end who needed to feel safe and I could do that.

Our family became very good at those emergency placements and I am so proud of my kids for handling it the way they did as young as they were. It changed the dynamic of our family at such a young age for my two oldest girls. They see life so differently than others, even me. They always said yes to sharing a room, clothes, and toys.

They would wake up as little girls and say, "Mom, who are we helping today?"

It makes me bawl now just thinking about it. Man, what if we lived like that as regular old daily life living grownups?

So many mornings they would wake up after I had been in the ER all night or up with a child an investigator dropped off. They were always thrilled to welcome a new temporary family member. Kids get it. I am not sure where we screw it up for them most times, but they actually get it so early on. They have no boundaries to this kind of love.

The Hot Second Choice That Changed Everything

One of those late-night calls happened about three years into our foster experience. A baby had been taken into the hospital and needed emergency care. The call came in during the middle of the night. Terrible timing. We were in the process of moving homes in the next few days. In a breath, I said, "Yes," and was in the car headed to the hospital. I always prayed all the way there. I was always nervous because you literally never know what kind of situation you will find yourself in, and with every single one of those Hail Mary prayers, God showed up. And boy, did He show up that night.

The baby was the tiniest thing you ever did see. She was an eight-week-old baby. She almost didn't even look real. I took her home, and after a few hours, our lives changed forever. Everyone in our home fell full-on in love. It was temporary, but she was perfect. Days moved into weeks and as we learned more about her story, I felt nudged to do things differently this round. Her mom was incarcerated locally so I reached out to the warden for a visit. I met with her on Saturdays for a time until she would be released and begin to earn her rights back.

> It was a painful kind of ask from God. Here I was totally in love with this child while He was totally loving her incarcerated momma.

She needed someone to love her. So, I clumsily took on that role. God taught me so much. He humbled me in new ways. No one could understand our journey or connection. It was just God. I wish I could say that everything turned up rainbows, but this is real life. Soon after this momma was released from jail, real life started to happen for her all over again. We think we know another's struggle, but we can never relate to them until we walk in their exact shoes.

The story is both happy and sad. It is always sad when a child is not able to be reunited with a birth parent, just as it is sad for a foster mom to let them go. This time the story in the end was not reunification. It was not an option, but the birth mom and I had really learned to see each other during those weekend visits. When it came down to it, she knew she could not raise her daughter and asked that we take on the role. So, while there was great heartache for us all, we were gifted a beautiful responsibility to raise one of the true loves of my life.

We have had children come and go. Some go back to birth parents, or to a relative. Some move on to a better suited foster placement, and some have stayed with us forever. When I signed up for this gig, never in a million years would I think I would have five daughters. That was not my plan.

Honest Feels

You love and let go. Except sometimes the letting go feels as if it will kill you. It won't. It will however rip your heart out, throw it on the ground and then go into your closet and pull out every piece of designer clothing you have and set them ablaze in your living room on the new rug you saved up for years to buy….so…yeah.

Be a Dawn

Remember way back when I was telling you about Dawn? You know, the one who was all blah blah "all the perfect words" I needed to hear to act on becoming a foster parent? I hope you have a Dawn. I hope you are a Dawn. See, over the years she has become one of my very best peeps. She listens to all my crazy, (it helps that she is a psychiatrist) and she sits in it with me. She lives in a way that challenges me to be better and do more. She doesn't want any attention (exact opposite of me) and she just is who she is. We can go for days, and many times weeks without connecting, but it is always fine. We just pick up where we left off.

We can learn a lot from the Dawns in our lives. Her words as a virtual stranger were so honest and real. They caused me to rethink my life and family. I never wanted to be a foster mom. It was not on my to do list. Maybe it is not on yours, but maybe it is. Maybe you have been looking for a sign. Here it is. Maybe your "fostering" is leaving the crappy job, relationship, or starting that non-profit, or digging in to mentor a kid or help a widow or just stinking *be the change* in any way. It is all the same in the end. Be encouraged, my people. Your words give life to others. You might be the very reason another has the guts to do the thing, whatever it is. Just when we think we have life kind of mapped out, I say, "Hold on," because it is likely about to be shaken up.

In case you need a visual, this is a pretty good example of the way we do life together. "Hey, I'm buying a camper," I said. "Sounds cool," she said. And then we both had campers! "LIVE", we say!

CHAPTER 7
STAND BY ME OR AT LEAST SEMI-CLOSE

Before you start skimming the next few pages, I want to say this chapter is for everyone: married, single, divorced and whatnot. My own personal experience, in a nutshell, includes taking a stab at the marriage game. I realize more and more as I become very honest, not all marriages are created equal. Some of us are legitimately more jacked than others. We can blame it on childhood or bad decisions prior to holy wedlock. I have no answers, just a story. Maybe this is a great spot to quote a bunch of stats on marriage, but it's just not my style. I never care what others did or did not do. We are all living on a wing and a prayer anyway, so I am considering it one more hallelujah that God has kept my holy union intact since 1997.

Side note: It was just a few weeks ago I thought I might have to re-write this chapter. So to be clear, this is not a chapter on marriage advice.

Let's talk about Beck (Eric), my fabulous overachieving husband. I refer to him over and over as a rock star because he is just that. Do I give him nearly enough credit in life, or show him nearly enough respect? That would be a NO. Right. We are decades in, and I'll be damned if I can sort out his love language. I mean, I know what he needs. Most men need to know we respect them and are proud of them. I got it.

Except I don't. I mean I DON'T got it, not I DON'T respect him. See how words can go there? They get me in a whole slew of trouble. I was raised radically different than Beck. My love language is kind of obvious. It is gifts. I know. I am the person with the horribly vain love language. Y'all, I am trying to keep it real so try not to judge me. I'm not a 'diamonds are a girl's best friend' kind of chick. I am more like, 'Hey bring me a Diet Dr. Pepper from my fave place and life is about to get super sweet for you' kind of gal.

Beck and I have known each other since we were twelve. Crazy sidebar…his mom met me right around the same time she was working for my family's business. She actually went home one night and told him she met the girl he was going to marry one day. You guys, this is a true story! We were not even buddies back then.

On A Winger and A Prayer

Soon enough fate brought us together when Beck got tickets to a Winger/Bullet Boys concert. Oh yes, we did. (Whatever, it was 1989.) I invited myself to one of his tickets and we became friends. Friends eventually melded into dating in high school. Sister, it was a love/hate relationship from day one. I basically lived to torture him. It seems though he had some memorable moments himself.

I remember one time he and his best bud stood me and my best girl up for a homecoming dance. I had my bangs as high as the sky, you guys. I was probably high on the hairspray fumes. We waited so patiently for the guys to come pick us up after the football game. There I was, looking like a 90's version Madonna wanna be, and there he was…not showing up.

Needless to say, things did not look good for him after that night. I was forced to go to the dance with no date where I had to dance with all of his friends. 'Cause that is what girls do. Little did I know, he was not looking forward to public dancing. So, he decided to drink lots of beers with his buddy instead. Good times.

The next Monday back at school, the guys decided to try to make amends. I was still hot. So, so hot. If looks could kill, I was on my way to Folsom Prison. It is funny the stuff we do that turns out to be a total fail. Beck and his sidekick, Mike, went to what I'm sure was the local gas station and bought some flowers, carnations to be exact. The game plan was to put the flowers on the windshield of both my and my girlfriend's cars in hopes of a romantic makeup. My friend went to her car, saw the flowers, and immediately went and made out with her guy. Boom. Success.

Here is where my side of the story differs from Beck's. Now, I will go with his story because I tend to make stuff bigger than it is. I saw the flowers on my windshield, looked around to see all the guys watching and waiting for the big win. I grabbed those crappy flowers and threw them on the ground. And as legend would have it, I spun out Dukes of Hazard style on those flowers in my little Geo Storm while simultaneously flying the guys the bird. Peace Out. *Also, carnations are pretty crappy flowers. Duh.

A Good Old College Try-ish

Chaos was pretty much a pattern we continued until college. It was just a week into rush at Mizzou, where we both decided to go to college, when it all came to a final end. We both had a taste of college life and decided to call it quits. I always laugh when people think we have been together since we were high school sweethearts. We were anything but sweet.

The next year in college was a little more of a blur for me than him. My party switch got turned up to the maximus while life slowly became way out of control. As much as I was losing Jesus, Eric was finding Him. I would be doing the walk of shame home from a fraternity close by as Eric would be walking to bible study. Wow did life take a different turn.

I went on to highly impress the parents by failing out of college. They were strict and swiftly over my shenanigans. I moved back to our local community and Eric stayed successful. See? He is usually winning at life.

I continued to unravel.

I took some pretty serious twists and turns in life over the next few years. It is a true statement that Eric and I both considered marrying other people. We both had serious relationships with good people. They were just not the right people. Though we had lost contact with each other, no one could quite measure up in either of our minds. I guess he could see the true good in me all along.

You guys, I'm still totally laughing, thinking about our high school telenovela. I was sure I was one of the only girls in my class not having sexual relations my junior and senior year. My mom had somehow put the fear of God in me, or maybe my shorts to be more specific. I was sure I was going Southern Baptist style, straight to Hades if I had sex before marriage.

I am really dissecting that learning style now since I am raising five girls…*hello*. I thought that mindset was messed up for years. Even though, I'm considering reviving it for my own kids. I mean they are already all set for a life in therapy, what's another layer gonna hurt?

Anywho, let's get back to our life many years later. Eric had gone on to rock it out in college and I went on to bomb it out in college. A series of less than savory decisions had me back in a town close to home figuring out how to do life.

A Christmas Miracle

A random Christmas Eve service brought us back together in our hometown. He was even more fab than I remembered. It was love at first sight all over again. Soon after, we decided to go slow and start dating again.

So, by this time, I had experienced life outside of morals when it came to dating. Now I was again dating Eric. He had found Jesus in a new and different way. I was stunned. No kissing, no PDA (public display of affection). Maybe a side hug, but that is as gritty as it was going to get. Wow. He decided he could not say 'I love you' until he knew I was the one he was to marry. You guys, I was a mess. As much as I had found God in my own way, I was always putting Beck to the test on the PDA. Needless to say, we were married in about a year.

I guess there is truly no way to prepare one for the realities of married life. Even as I sit here and write, my five kids are screaming in the pool. I am blown away by the fact that Beck and I are still going strong after decades of marriage. I will say it again...believe in miracles!

Marriage – The Modern-Day Lion's Den

I kind of want to hug girls a little too tight when they tell me with bright eyes that they are getting married. I kind of also want to whisper in their ear, *Run like hell!* Before you read me as a total cold-hearted snake (shout out to Paula Abdul), I just feel a sadness maybe left over from this time in my own life. I felt like I was a very sub-par wife.

Bringing together the realities of two damaged people is dangerous. Does that mean everyone is damaged? Of course not. But I'm living in this mind and I can only see what I see, and I have three VW vans worth of baggage I seem to never be able to totally unload.

I know and have heard that there are plenty of people who have perfect weddings and go on to bliss out in marriage. In my heart of hearts, I don't think it is true, which is even more messed up. But please try to love me through this, one of my many flaws. My first three years of marriage were a blur. I always seemed to be unhappy or maybe looking for something I could never exactly find.

Eric and I communicated totally differently, and still do, to this day. I had basically zero communication skills. He had dominated all kinds of therapy prior to us getting married. I believed therapy was for sissies and I ain't no sissy. (Keep in mind this was before thousands of dollars were spent sorting my own life out in the relaxing chair of a therapist). It is easier to blame. I was awesome at it. I'm not sure I ever played the victim card, but I could seriously manipulate our situation when needed.

Sometimes I wonder why he stayed married to me. I was sure he would leave. If I am being totally honest, I probably pushed him as hard as I could at times just to prove my theory. I was sure for years (and by years, I mean even now most times) I could make Eric more like me. Lord knows I have it all figured out. Here I am a big, full-size baby woman about half the time. I want what I want.

I have discovered that I am a teensy part introvert. Now this has been a hard realization for me as I swear, I am 1000% extrovert. Because extroverts are the most fun and I want to be the most fun already. For some reason that feels weak to admit. But let me tell you, and apparently myself, introverts are *strong*.

Now, I am married to a radical extrovert. This guy does not meet a stranger. I have seen him win over the biggest turd burglars (thank my kids for that one). Before we got married, I thought that was so hot. I mean, I loved how he would roll in and be the center of attention. People loved him. I have people tell me all the time what an outgoing and kind person he is. You guys, he is THE man.

While I loved his outgoing personality before marriage, once we were married, my insecurities started to slowly leak out. I would try to shut him down. Maybe I felt like he was talking for too long to someone, or maybe it was that he was so comfortable talking to others that I felt left out. I am still trying to crack that nut all these years later.

We are a good combo of crazy, I will admit. I am not saying we ever did this…umm…but we could be a pretty bad to the bone wedding crashing couple. I have an overactive imagination as I have been told and Eric is fearless in the communication department. He is also one of the most honest guys I know. So, lying for him seems to be impossible, while I could literally live a double life, and no one would know, but don't worry, I am not…as far as you know.

I need to say this since I sounded like such a jerk earlier. I love newlyweds. I want to see you win. I want to see you prove my old mindset wrong. I have to believe my kids will do that for me. I'm rooting for you. And guess what? Life is hard and anything worth something takes serious work. So, we work. We forgive. We give do overs.

Guys need us to respect them. And here I am telling my man he needs to tone himself down. What the hell is wrong with me? See, it all makes sense as I write it. I think now, *Why would I ever do that?* But then life creeps back in and I do it all over again.

Eric used to be a total rule follower. I was the rebel. In most cases I still am, but now he is too, which causes problems. I think about the time I became a mom, I went safe. Rules. I'm gonna spitball this one, but I'm guessing it was because I was so far out of my comfort zone. As the kids kept coming, my rules started growing, which I hated because that is not my nature at all. I swear I am the fun one.

Here is one instance where I successfully changed Eric and it totally backfired for me. I remember Pre-K (you will see this randomly, it means pre-kid in my world), Beck had the nicest car. He always had something that looked straight off the showroom floor. My car would look much different, but I am positive a lot of fun was being had in it.

I would get into Eric's car with my drink, shove it in the drink carrier and within minutes could feel the tension growing. No words need be exchanged. That dang cup would start to sweat and then drip water (heaven forbid) into its cup holder. Guys Yeti was not a thing back then. It was only a matter of time until Beck's undies were in such a twist you won't care to imagine. Sweaty cup…in the cup holder…what might happen? I tormented him with my witty banter about his Type A ways that were really just passive aggressive moments presented as humor. Over time, Eric got a good grasp on his extreme ways. I just kept being my messed-up self because clearly, I was fine.

While We are on the Subject, How About We Talk About Sex?

Uh…sorry, mom. What a mess. I am sure most of you have a "Fifty Shades" kind of sex lives, so you might not understand. Now, let me reveal myself as even less cool when I say I have never even seen that movie or read the books.

I started to watch the movie late one night on TNT or some channel that was censored and I felt a hot wave of guilt come over me. It was definitely a hot wave for sure. I'm gonna go with guilt.

What-evs, I know better than to plant seeds like that in my head. So as cool as I wanna be in relating to everyone's modern ways, I am just not that cool. I don't need to add to my already crazy thought life. Don't worry though, I am not judging you for it, 'cause remember, this is a No Judgement Zone.

Here we are all these years in and sex is still an odd place for us. It is like something we need to schedule. I don't know. I am not even sure I can write about it, but I want to write about it because no one is honest about it. I guess five kids play into the whole game. You guys, my bedroom door has not been locked in years. My little kids like to hang like wild animals; upside down from the door handles, hence no locks, therefore nothing is sacred in my boudoir.

Future Therapy Topics

You can really scar a kid for life. I remember years ago when we were in a Barry White kind of moment in our old house only to be quietly "interrupted" by my two older kids standing in the doorway. That's super fun to explain. I guess life is really just a series of messing up our kid's minds one act at a time.

I don't really feel 'hot' most times. I mean, I feel more like a science exhibit when I am just trying to get ready, or freaking bathe myself, only to look up and have several sets of eyes staring at my lady parts. We have a rule about this which no one seems to follow! Stay outta my bathroom! They break it. Every. Single. Day.

I think age is an evolution in all things. Some of you are having sex like rock stars with the hubs. Some of us are kicking butt at being at peace with where we are. Others of us are still wondering if we are doing it right. No matter how tweaked my brain gets or how distant our marital union becomes, we have some ground rules that we typically don't budge from.

Never leave. That means you can be madder than mad. You can go to the opposite end of the house and not speak for a day, but no one leaves the other. This is to protect my old dad wounds from taking root in my marriage.

Always sleep in the same bed. This is a biggie. I am not even sure where it all started but we agreed. You can still be angry but at the end of the day, we choose each other.

One other thing that I basically stink at 80% of the time is doing our best to *live by the 1 Corinthians challenge on what Love is*:

"Love is patient, love is kind. It does not envy, it does not boast, it is not proud. It does not dishonor others, it is not self-seeking, it is not easily angered, it keeps no record of wrongs. Love does not delight in evil but rejoices with the truth. It always protects, always trusts, always hopes, always perseveres" (NIV, 1 Cor. 13:4-8).[2]

Right.

You guys, those words. In our marriage, we are challenged to always go back to insert our names in place of the word love and read it from there as a barometer on how we are doing.

Way to kick us right square in the important parts. Sometimes I just want to do the blaming. I will say, however, over the years I have learned to apologize and also forgive like a boss. God has released me in so many ways. On the flip side, if there is anyone I will hold a grudge with, it is Eric. He is my person. I think I do it with him more than anyone else because I know he is going to stick around until I get over myself. We drive each other crazy, love each other radically, and are both extremely passionate people. Of course, he is my safe place for all my peculiar ways to play out.

We are becoming gentler with each other as we get older. Never be mistaken though, as much as we work toward goodness, there will always be a force working against us. A force that is moving me to be selfish. A nudge to cause him to close off his affection.

> Marriage is a constant battle for love to win.

I hope you win. Whether you are happily married, unenthusiastically married and barely hanging on, single, divorced, in a relationship, whatever it is; if you love someone, fight for them. Amazing things don't typically come easy. You can mess up. You can give each other a break. You can choose to forgive, and by forgive, I mean let it completely go, the way God forgives us. This is a tough one.

We tend to keep a running tab on our loved ones' screw-ups. Realize we all have weak spots and agree to give grace in them. But hear me loud and clear girls, _abuse is a whole other story_. In no case should you apply these words in situations of abuse. If you feel like you might be in a relationship that feels dangerous or unpredictable, or your gut is just kinda nagging you about it…please, please, TELL SOMEONE. ANYONE.

Our marriage has been a work in progress since day one of a LOT of years. I do not claim to have much of anything figured out, other than it is hard work and when it is good, it is amazing. There is no one in the world who knows me better, has my back, or supports me more than this guy. Through thick and thin, literally and figuratively, he is always willing to stand by me…or at least fairly close.

CHAPTER 8
YOU BETTER CHECK YO' SELF
BEFORE YOU WRECK YO' SELF

Have you ever had one of those defining moments in life when maybe you made a phenomenal choice and it paid off brilliantly? Okay, well this story is kind of the opposite of that kind of decision. I stewed over even writing about it because it was such a stinking bad move. I still look back and wonder what the heck I was ever thinking. Life has a way of really taking a turn now and then. About four years ago, to the exact day I am writing this, I got a call. It was not the kind of call I would have ever expected in one thousand years.

Let me set the scene so you know what sort of situation we were dealing with.

So, there I was in the heart of foster parenting. By that I mean I had five kids in the house under the age of eight. It was legit crazy town in our house. I can think back now and feel the exact feelings I felt back then. My days ran together, and pretty much every day I wore the same pair of pants…always…black leggings as you might imagine. So, when body parts swelled, it was less noticeable. Let it be known, I am a stress eater. I had three kids in diapers, and I felt like I was invisible. Make sure you read that correctly I said *invisible* not invincible. Can you relate? I would go to church and hope someone would see that I was hanging on by a thread. But like I said earlier, most times, they would just ooh and ahh over the fact we all made it to church and we were, "doing such a good thing for these kids".

What thing was that exactly?

If they only knew.

Also add to pretty much every conversation a blatant awkwardness which no one is to blame for because it is confusing to know what is ok to ask with foster families. (Although I will be happy to give you some guidelines, as you might expect).

Diapers and Dry Shampoo

I was short-tempered and blurry-eyed. I was bathing maybe twice a week. My hair took on its own formation most days and I was continually trumping myself on days gone without washing it. Dry shampoo was severely abused on a regular basis. I crossed paths with Eric randomly a few times a day in the midst of diaper changes and taking out the trash, but that was pretty much it. We were in deep.

I had moments where I was proud of myself and felt like the sacrifice was right. If I had more sleep, I would have probably felt like that more frequently, but it was hit or miss most days. One of our foster babies would cry during the night. It was a miserable cry. It would go on and on and was totally inconsolable. I hated it for him. I would prop us both up while I held him and pray that God would give him some comfort. I loved this little dude. He had clearly stolen my heart. So, I was all in even though I was unable to make really solid decisions during that period of life due to severe lack of sleep.

> Sometimes people say, "God will never give you more than you can handle." Hear me friend. That is a lie from the pit.

Not that I am saying people are liars, however, I stand firmly in the place that people are severely misled in this particular thought life. The truth, at least my truth, is that God has led me down some radical paths in life. I have also taken myself down some crazy paths. For real. Both sides.

At this point we were fostering a little fella, twelve months, a baby girl, fourteen months, our Ari age three, Solie age six and Bianca was age eight. I need to remind you here, my forte has never been organization. I told you how my home was structured earlier in the book.

I was just trying to find socks. That is all I was doing those days. Looking for the dang blasted socks and shoes, and changing diaper after diaper, and filling up all things landfill. I'm sorry, future generations.

Who's Calling on a Sunday?

One random Sunday, THE call came in. All of the kids were down for a nap and I clearly remember being laid flat out on the living room floor. My cell phone was ringing with a call from none other than the woman that got me into all this wonderful fostering mess in the first place. It was Dawn. Now, I knew something major was up because anyone who knows and loves me never calls unless it is uber important. So, if after reading this book, you decide we are going to be besties 'cause I am so magnetic and all, go ahead and get it in your Cliff's Notes now: "Momma does not like to talk on the phone". I have an emoji for everything, so you can plan ahead to text all life events to me, or just text me alerting me that we need to meet in real-life person.

Anyway, back to the call. Dawn is on the other end asking me about one of my baby's birth moms. This is the birth momma I told you a bit about earlier. We had gotten to know each other early on. I soon learned on that life-altering call, this same bio momma had just given birth to a bouncing baby girl. Full stop. Re-read that sentence. *No one knew this was coming, on the radar, in the works…nada.*

She just had a baby girl. Now let me give you a little 411 of fostering. We had a baby girl (this surprise new baby's sister) who had been with us for over a year. All signs pointed to adoption. Ya know, the baby that totally stole our heart after being in our home for like five minutes? We were literally just a handful of months away from a court date to make it official. Any time you have a kiddo in your home and a bio mom has another child that will come into foster care, the state will do all things possible to keep bio siblings together. I totally understand the reasoning on this, by the way. Of course, kids should be together. Yes. The very least they deserve is to be together when all the other parts of life are unpredictable.

Now, at the point where I got this call, I was not in the mental space to receive it. The baby would be in the hospital for a few days but then would need a foster home, which pointed directly to this girl (me).

Cluttered and Semi-Sanitary

I feel like right about here I should write some run-on sentence about what a blessing it would in fact be to host another baby child in our cluttered up semi-sanitary home where daily I seemed to misplace at least one of these baby children for a hot second… like a huge blessing, and how could I not say yes because God had given me such a wonderful responsibility…now with another opportunity to give yet another child a loving home 'cause everyone needs to have four diaper wearers at once in a house with only one large trash can in the kitchen. Yes, I know that is not up to health code, thank you very much.

But I won't write that run on sentence. Wink.

I remember hearing all the words and hanging up. No emotion until 3,2,1…whammo. I b-lined to our bedroom to drop the situation on Eric. I know I have shared a fair amount about his awesome self, but occasionally, his responses still floor me. "Hmm…so you are saying we are going to have another baby."

All statement, no question. Uh…noooo! I am not up for this in any manner.

Even that pride part of me that screams out, "I am Super Woman. Can't you see I do it all? Why would I not do this?"

Yeah, that girl had long left the building. I think she might have been asleep on someone's patio furniture down the street. You might be thinking, *just say no and move on.* Except it is much more complicated. We had a bio sibling in our care already. The sibling to said baby newborn.

Remember earlier when I said the state would keep bio siblings together? Well, even though we were so close to adopting the sibling, we still risked the state moving the child we had to be with the baby, should we not take the new baby placement. Does this even make sense? It is a lot to follow, friends, I get it.

Maybe I need to insert a diagram right about here, but I suck at all the art drawing kinds of things.

When to Say, "When"?

So, there we were with a decision to make. I knew I would tip right off the edge into a nervous breakdown if we took this baby. I was positive 1000% that I could not handle it, which is big because I never admitted weakness back then. I began making plans in my own head. I got on the phone with one of my other besties, Tracie. Tracie and I had been through all the tough things in life together. We became friends when I wrote her a note the summer of our seventh-grade year asking to be friends. It was a check the box yes or no kind of situation.

Of course, we became fast friends and we both played the alto sax together in the Dexter Bearcub Marching Band. (Definitely try to find a CD of that middle school collaboration if you get a chance.) She has seen me do all kinds of things that would make people run for the hills. I guess the time I tested her in my earliest memory was when she saw me pick my nose in band class and put it under my seat. I thought I was doing it on the down low only to look up and lock eyes with her. She could have ruined me and my band reputation right at that moment. Now, she did have a solid laugh over it, but she never told anyone.

Go get that kind of friend in your life. Friends that keep your boogers a secret. She could and should have totally humiliated me over it, but she probably knew I would lie about it anyway. Then some truth seeker would have turned the chair upside down to check for evidence and that would have been the end of my semi-cool middle school status.

We have been through gigantic hair and proms. She lived with us for a bit in high school. Really, the list never ends. Tracie is that person that I can say all of the really dumb stuff to and she does not hold it against me. Maybe she is a stuffer, which is dandy in my book because I need friends who act like I don't drive them crazy even when I do.

Help a Sister Out

So, once I decided I could not take on this newborn baby, I called Tracie. She could do it. I knew she would be perfect. She was a rock star mom. She could raise this baby and since we are practically sisters, I would raise the sibling (the baby's sister I already had) and we would basically still have them as family. *I did not say it was a sane plan, but I didn't have much to work with at the time in my own head.*

I don't even really know how it came about, but Tracie decided that, in fact, she would talk to her husband and this might be an option. Wow, it was all kind of happening fast. In my gut, which I heavily ignored, something was off. I had to keep extra busy trying not to think about the whole situation. I spent hours calling in favors to sell my idea to all the potential people who would be involved in the decision making. I felt sick.

A day or so after the initial call, we found out that this new baby girl had a heart defect. Ugh. Now I knew for sure I could not handle it. Talk about adding all the wrong ingredients to the mix. We were maxed out. All the while as I was talking a lot and nudging and pushing everyone else, I had my own nudging and pushing going on. I had to deal with it mostly at night. I could not sleep. I was miserable in my spirit. I knew what God was asking of me. He was very clear. The more I ignored Him the more persistent He was.

It was just a handful of days until my BFF had her heart totally in to take on this baby girl. She was talking cribs and details, and her kids were even excited. Every time I heard her voice and the anticipation in it, I wanted to run. It was like a train wreck happening in slow motion just outside of my reach.

Eric knows me so well. He kept quiet for the most part until one day when I was making dinner, he overheard me on the phone working out this child's future. I could tell he was disgusted. He asked me what I thought I was doing. I ignored him. He replied that it seemed like I was trying to be in control in spite of God. I was so mad because he was so right.

Playing God

I looked him right in the face and lied to him. I told him that God had not in fact told me to take the baby and I was just doing my best to help. I think he knew I was lying but I was so angry I pretty much shut him down completely. I did not need his advice. I would be the one who was taking on another baby for the most part, and frankly, I did not want his input or his stinking observation. (Now, to be clear I was just in 'poor me' mode. He is such an interactive dad. I was just being a jerk and knew his truth was messing with me.) He is an eternal optimist. Some days I love it. Some days I want to tell him to stick it. (Then I refer myself back to that dang "Love is…" scripture.)

The process to "rehome new baby" was in full effect. Calls were made, agendas were pushed. Somehow, I was able to use my persuasive mouth to get all the right people on board with this new arrangement. So, I had totally steam rolled everyone. I got my best friend on the line to mom this new baby. I was able to have all the right people give it a nod to make it happen when it actually made very little sense. It was just the timing. Our system was and still is busting at the seams with kids needing placement. I guess this seemed like a decent enough idea in the heat of the situation.

I tried to think very little about the bio sisters who would not actually grow up in the same house due to my selfishness. Thinking about it made me feel a sickness I haven't found words in the dictionary for. God was in my face all the time reminding me this was my plan and not His. I could not sleep or eat, but I was moving ahead.

As my doubts grew in equal measure, so did the excitement of my bestie and her family at the prospect of adding a baby to their family.

I was in so ridiculously far over my head. The baby had been in the hospital for a week while they learned a bit more about her heart situation. It gave us time. We needed time to sort out her future.

One morning about a week in, I woke up and I could no longer bear the load that was crushing me. No one knew. I had told not one word to anyone, and, guys, I am a talker. I am a feeler. Usually everyone in the room is crystal clear on how I feel, stranger or otherwise. It was like a dam that was about to break. I thought I was having a nervous breakdown. I was hot and cold and stir crazy. I could not have a regular conversation with anyone, and I sort of hoped I would spontaneously combust. In my mind, temporarily, I thought it would be better if I was gone.

> I was running from God, but He kept finding me. He never lost sight of me, and His persistence was making me crazy.

It was just a handful of days prior when I spoke out loud, "I know what you want God and I cannot do it. I won't do it. I am sorry, but it is too much. So, find someone else. I am out."

From those words, life seemed to spiral out of control. I was lying to all of the people around me who loved me. It was suffocating. My go-to people were family members who thought I was clearly above my pay grade on this situation already, without adding another child. I found it easier to live my lie around them. So, I clung to their sympathetic words and feedback of what I already felt. *I was doing enough.*

The Truth Shall Set This Girl Free

The day the dam broke, I called my mom and Eric's mom. His mom was right across the street, so I could get to her first. I needed to see them both. Now keep in mind, Eric remained oblivious. As far as he knew, the deal is done. We are not taking this baby.

My mom was stunned when I asked her to get in the car and come as quickly as she could. She had an hour drive. She made it in 45 minutes. I talked to Eric's mom first. Everything came out. I felt sick and relieved and a tiny bit less like leaving my life. She cried with me and knew what the weight of these words meant for our family. My mom was next. I lost all control when I saw her. She had been so encouraging of my original decision when I could not handle it.

Oh, girls, I hope you get to have a mom in your life. I get to have two and I am so grateful. My mom's face was so sincere when I melted down in front of her. I told her everything, how I had lied and lied and lied and had been running from God and basically telling Him to stick it and find a new situation. She also knew the deep love I had for my best friend and realized the damage I would do in telling her the truth. I tried to breathe, and she just listened. I knew what I had to do. I had to come clean. I had to tell everyone the truth and I would hurt people immensely because of my actions. It was one of the hardest days of my life.

I had to tell my friend. I remember texting her. She knew something was up but had no clue what I was about to drop on her. I showed up at her house. I was raw and honest and a total mess. She just looked at me. It took a while to sink in. Wait. I had put this whole plan together. I got her on board and super pumped to add a new family member. Her family had their hearts in it. I had worked the system and steered every possible conversation to go the way I wanted and here we were. Not to mention my sweet husband had no clue.

The moments in front of Tracie felt like hours as I let it all out. She was devastated. I wondered how in the world she would ever find it in her heart to forgive me. I mean, I had screwed up before in our long sisterhood, but nothing even in this galaxy could compare. I remember hugging her and wondering if it would be the last time. You guys, she is not a crier, and she was crying. That was not a good sign. I was such a screw up. I hated myself in those moments but also felt a little more like I could breathe a tiny bit.

Surprise

I asked Eric to meet me at the hospital right after. He thought we were going to pray for healing for the baby. I met him in the parking lot, and I know I looked like a crazy person. I had been crying for hours at this point. I still had to tell him.

Hi honey. Remember how I told you there was no way in hell we were taking this baby? Well…surprise!

Okay, it did not go quite like that…like, at all. I had to pull him aside and tell him I had been lying to him for over a week. I wish that on no one, by the way. It is a horrible feeling. So, do yourself a favor and don't be a liar. See? You are winning already.

I have never really lied to Eric up to that point. I mean, I would consistently be vague on how much money I spent at Nordstrom, but that was it. Other than that, I was always just a blunt and sarcastic open book. When I told him I had been lying, he said he already knew. He could see me unraveling but he loved me enough to let me figure it out. Wow. He is such a bigger person than me.

So, in that hospital parking lot, I dropped a bomb of bombs. We were not there to pray for the baby but to become her caregivers and potentially parents, long term.

Even as we made our way up to the hospital NICU, it was so obvious that Eric was totally in. He was calm and excited, and I was needing a cocktail. I had just likely lost my best friend and added a child to an already stressful home situation. A nurse took a photo of us that day and I keep it super handy on my phone at all times to never forget how I felt.

We took baby girl home just a few days after that life-altering morning. It was a total game changer.

And as for Tracie, she decided to stay with me. It was hard and awkward and uncomfortable, but she stuck. She knew I could not do this on my own and she made the decision to forgive me in spite of all the pain I caused her. She stayed. I could not believe it. She channeled her heartache into service. We can all learn from her. Have people in your life like Tracie. People who stick and never give up on you when you are at your absolute worst. They say life takes a village and there are no truer words. She served our family as did so many others.

Living Proof

Very few people know the details of this story up until this point. I have felt a good deal of shame about it. You know that we are already tough on ourselves as women, but royally screw up at life? It tends to haunt you. It has haunted me. I understand now that is the enemy plain and simple. He is always trying to pick out our insecurities and make us feel less…smaller than we actually are. As long as we feel small, we play small. We are trapped. We have all of this truth to share with the world to help them get free and we are scared to death of what people will think if they find out who we actually are.

So, here I sit three years later taking that one baby step to freedom. It truly is like when a baby decides crawling is for sissies and decides to use those two long appendages to do something more than drag behind her body. She stands. She is wobbly and unsure until one day she gathers her confidence up enough to put that one chubby leg out in front of the other, and from there it is gang busters. Maybe that is what God wants for us. I am getting deep here, but as long as we are crawling, we can't run free.

I have done one crappy thing after another to screw up my life in certain seasons. This is just one of the more painful choices. To decide full-on I would walk away from God was a dangerous choice I hope you never choose to make after reading this. Tons of pain resulted in my decisions in those days. Even though Eric totally forgave me, it was hard on our already strained marriage. It took massive damage control to rebuild my friendship. And one day I will have to tell my beautiful baby girl that momma was just so selfish at one point, I almost missed her. Not to mention I almost ignored her need to be with her big sister. Man, that burns my eyes just writing those words. Consequences are a beast.

Now I have that baby girl as my daughter. Our unexpected plus one. She runs our house and has been very appropriately named Baby Boss. She and her bio sister, who is also now our daughter, are like twins. They are fourteen months apart and totally inseparable.

It turns out, our choices affect everything. So, if you are reading this and thinking about how much you have screwed something up, have hope. God can work it out in spite of us. Sometimes it doesn't happen nice and tidy, but it can happen. I am living proof.

The day it all shook down. Eric looking fresh as a flower and me looking like I had been hit by a bus.

CHAPTER 9
GIRL, GO LIVE ALREADY!

So, in case it seems like I am screaming from the rooftop, "Girl, go live!" I am. I am standing out here in the morning chill with my coffee sans bra in this old robe screaming at the top of my written word voice…YOU ARE WORTH IT! Now GO DO THE THING! Please know I am saying that with all the love I have in my heart, and my heart is giant. The truth is, going all in and living life without fear is scary. There is risk. There is a lot of risk, and likely pain involved. Now, doesn't that sound tempting?

I have lived on both sides. I have told my fears to suck it, and I have lived out loud. I have also gotten into bed and pulled the covers over my head for a season…or seven. It is a constant battle.

I was talking to my girlfriends just this morning as we were trying to help one of them decide if she was going to take the leap and quit her job. The timing stunk. If she could only work a few more months, years…whatever. But God was nudging her to leap. And that is exactly what He asks most of the time. The timing can stink. The timing will usually stink! That is why it is called faith, my friend!

Ugh, if only it could be wrapped up in a big pink bow with an ice-cold Diet Dr. Pepper right beside it. God asks us to take the step *before* there is a step. Then He makes a way. You know, the way we cannot see until we take the step…and only then one more step appears…instead of the stairway… 'cause that would just be too easy. It's so easy to feel every single weakness and run every horrible scenario through our mind five hundred times, but God wants us to know HE is enough.

The Super Sister

Have you ever felt like you are not enough? Like, maybe even in the last five minutes? Uh, yeah, me too. I think back to when it all started. I have so many memories of how I have not been enough through the years. I think back to when I was a kid, and my sister and I used to sing at church. So, my sister is all that and a bag of Doritos. I mean she was the ultimate do everything, be in everything, and sing like Beyonce kind of sister. I am almost four years younger and I always felt like I never would measure up to her awesomeness. Funny how a young girl's brain can work.

We used to go to my family holidays in Kentucky where a whole slew of my beautiful girl cousins would join us. They were all significantly older than me, but I felt they were untouchable. As I danced my way awkwardly into good old puberty, I hit a growth spurt. For some reason, everyone on that side of my family seems to be short. So, when I would show up at these family get-togethers, all the beautiful cousins talked about how tall I was. Instead of totally owning my gazelle like nature, I hunched down and felt big. Did you hear that? I felt *big*. You guys. I am 5'6". It is not like I am in the WNBA. I am a totally regular height, but I felt huge in the midst of all the petite, pretty people.

Over the years, I continued to hunch down from subconsciously not wanting to be big. I did not even realize it. I am 45 and I still have to make myself stand up straight. If you look at almost any photo of me growing up and into adulthood, I have a bit of a slump. Now that is *cray cray*, but it is what I came to believe in my soul. A thing that was a total lie from the pit of hell. See how easy just one comment that is spoken innocently can sit in a young girl's mind? (So, if you are raising girls, God help you. This is a reminder we have no clue what is going on in their head.)

My sister is everything to me. She is still the most amazing singer I know. So, when I was young, I would have to sing duets in church with her, little Whitney Houston junior. Imagine that. Regular voice girl who is also doubling as a giant-singing southern gospe-tality with a perfect tiny song bird sister. What the h-e-double-hockey-sticks?

I was young and kind of looking forward to my sister growing up and getting out of the house. She had been stealing my thunder long enough. She was just as ready to move on to bigger things. Then finally, she left for college and it was my time to shine. My insecurities grew along with my height. I was still asked to sing at my childhood church. I would do it, but not without a ton of anxiety. If only we said out loud what we feel. Or what if we had a neon light that flashed above our heads with our personal truths. Man, would that change the world we live in; our own personal honesty veils.

Here is what my honesty veil would flash as I sang at church on any given Sunday:

I know you think my voice kinda sucks. And yes, I am Candy's little sister. I know you are all tear drops that she went on to college and now you are forced to listen to me attempt to sing.

Or, maybe as time marched on when I was a senior in high school and totally lost…

I am totally hung over right now. I can hardly remember the words because my head hurts so bad.

Uh…for that last one especially, please try not to judge me, church friends. I think back about the decisions I made in high school and wonder why in the world God carried me through all of them in spite of myself. Our group of girlfriends drank all of the time. We lived in a very small town and the ultimate thrill was trying to buy beer on the weekends. Looking back, it was nuts. I guess now that I am a mom, my mind is kind of blown thinking about it. I drove most weekends under the influence. I have horrible regrets of what could have been. And even with all of the crazy thoughts that ran through my head, God was still working.

He never gives up on us. He will never give up on you. In case you need to read these words right now, God is telling me to put them right here:

> You are enough. Actually, you are kinda perfect. Not perfect like the world perceives perfect, but perfect as God created you to be. Perfect in the sense that you are made exactly as he planned. Maybe you feel like you are not measuring up. Maybe you wonder if God could ever really forgive your sins. Maybe you are sure you are doing a crappy job at raising humans, or spreading God's love, or any other possible (fill in the blank) out there.

> Hear this. God loves you as you are. We get grace renewed every single day. When He forgives us, He wipes our slates clean. And unlike humans, He has no memory of our wrongdoings. We are His kids. He wants us to win. He wants us to feel loved. We are Daughters of the King, my friends. There is no perfect!

Ease Up Already

I have no clue why in the world we are so dang hard on ourselves as women. Could we all just agree to stop this already? Maybe we need an incentive because surely our own impending freedom is not enough. For those of us who have kids, uh, you know what I'm about to drop here. We are teaching our kids so much more by the way we live than the words from our mouths. Most of us are scared y'all...of so many things. Worry grips us. It smothers us. If we continually act and speak like we are not enough and live based in fear, our kids will learn the same for themselves. Hello…wake-up call times one billion!

If you are with a partner, or looking for a partner, or you could care less about a partner; unlocking your freedom can only begin with you. I'm guilty of looking at Eric and sometimes being jealous. I mean how can he do whatever he wants and not even worry about what everyone will think, who he will let down, and all the other blah, blah, blahs?

I think the weight of the issue in this area is on women for the most part. Do we have our fig leaf wearing girl Eve to blame? Yep. I'm blaming Eve for our raging insecurities as a woman culture. Maybe the people pleasing is a direct result of her biting into that forbidden fruit forevermore. I mean, let's face it, her decision impacted forever in a big way. If that forbidden fruit would have been a pizza or anything cake related, I would have been all over it too. Eve was the first example of a woman's own will kicking her in the lady parts.

So, of course the future of woman humanity would try to make up for it by doing all of the things, being all of the things, and putting ourselves completely LAST. Careful to care about what others think. So unsure about standing in our own radicalness. The constant battle to be content. (And Eve, if you are reading this, I would have likely done the same thing, so don't be beating yourself up, girl.)

> I want to be clear here, sisters. It is a war, not a battle. When we get right and say yes to God, get ready. It is no joke.

So while we may read books and watch tons of inspirational videos of feel good stories of people overcoming great odds, we must remember, these stories came at a cost and usually began with a war and it likely took place in a deep valley. The nod to God to go all in does not come without battle scars. I am not trying to scare anyone, but I have to be frank. It is not a situation where we say yes to God and life is all of a sudden sweeter and more pleasant and, "Why in the world didn't I do this before?" kind of deal. It is more like, "Hey girl, game on." So, we put on our big girl power pants and prepare for the journey of a lifetime.

Hey, Overcomer

Everyone loves to hear a story of overcoming, but guess what? There would be no story if there was not pain. I hope you are following me. We can choose to live a life without risk. It can feel semi safe and we can do our very best to avoid pain. But when we say yes to God, we have to know it will come with challenges. I will be honest with you. God has asked me to do some ridiculous stuff. One of the biggest I have not even touched on in this book. He has also asks me to do uncomfortable things pretty much every day when I am listening. Some days I do them and others I ignore him. I might as well write the truth here. It is not like God doesn't already know. So, if we are going to do this, let's do this.

Faith.

"Now faith is confidence in what we hope for and assurance about what we do not see" (NIV, Heb. 11:1).[3]

Whelp, there you go, girls. How do we ever truly dig into a life of faith without jumping into the deep end? Sure, life will give us the screws at some point no matter how safe we live, and we will fall on our knees to God…begging, pleading, negotiating. Been there and done that times a thousand.

How about when we make the choice to follow God? I will give you a fun little warning. Be careful what you pray for. I remember praying to God that He would increase my faith. For months, I prayed that God would grow my faith, on my knees with full church style reverence. Guess what? He totally answered my prayers in all the ways I did not want.

Be Careful What You Pray For

I guess that saying, "Be careful what you wish for" could apply like a boss right about here. How exactly did I believe in my vanilla mind that God would increase my faith? By filling up my bank account? By giving me flawless skin and marital bliss? Or maybe I would settle for a dewy youth-like complexion and 2.2 kids? God did not get that memo.

He went all Jesus of Nazareth on me and dropped me to my knees in a whole new way. Now, before you read this and think God put a bunch of horrible stuff in my life to teach me faith, you are right. Ha. I am kidding. Sort of. I don't want to get in a big debate over how God does stuff because I am not God. It is also way above my pay grade to have any business teaching anyone about why God does and allows what He does. I do, however, know exactly what He has allowed in my life to teach me gargantuan lessons when I have prayed this prayer:

God, I just want to trust You more…in everything I do. I don't want to be in control. I want You to lead my life. I give it to You.

Did anyone else feel the earth shake right after that prayer?

Oh, just me? So here is a sampling of what God did to answer my prayers....

He led us to adopt. As you learned in detail earlier in this book, He sorted me out in a major way. Did I learn to trust Him? Ummm... yes. I had zero control. I could fix nothing. All I could do was pray and guess what else? Trust Him. Was it painful at times? Yes, please. Was it completely mind shattering wonderful also? For sure.

Oh good, I learned that lesson. Increased faith? Check that box as DONE. Whew. Good thing I got past that, only to get thrown almost immediately into another uncertain international adoption. I had problems arise with my family for the decisions Eric and I made to follow God. It made others feel uncomfortable, like super uncomfortable. *Wait, you just finished an adoption. You know, the million-dollar baby? Again? So soon?*

Honestly, some of the people we love the most had reservations about us adopting an African child. Dang. That was hard. It was sad on so many levels and for so many reasons. It was anything but a sweet and simple time. We had to stand in our faith. And once we stood in our faith, we had to keep standing. God didn't just see that we were being faithful for a second and fix everything. We had to be strong. I cried a lot. I did a ton of retail therapy which helped for exactly zero seconds, but at least I looked fashionable as I was following the Lord. I am sure Nordstrom thanks me.

God took our Ethiopian adoption and changed lives in radical ways that prior to our saying *yes,* I didn't even know needed changing.

So, while we were all, "Wahoo, we are having another baby!"

God was all, "Let me change hearts and minds in people you have no idea need changing. I am God, okay? I am doing all the things you have no clue about."

Of course, these are just my thoughts of how it would go in the Big Man's mind.

When we ask, we better get our wading boots on. It's gonna get deep. But see, that is where our stories come from. Life gets really hard. We get really close to God. He does a thing in us and at some point, we heal a little and get a little stronger. It is not like one day we wake up and are all done with our process. We get to run and stay and all the things in between.

Constant Undoing

For me with each kid that came into my life, there was this crazy undoing. I fought it most of the time and every now and then during a rare moment, I embraced it. I was getting stripped down in areas of pride. Don't worry, they still creep up. I guess I can't seem to get enough of myself. We became foster parents. Never in a million was I going to be a foster mom, but there I was. The phone rang randomly for kids all of the time. At first you kind of feel all this pressure to take every kid they call about. It might be different in another part of the country but in our town, you will get called, a lot.

When you are going through the classes to foster and they are scaring the hell out of you every week, you get to decide what ages of kids you are willing to take. Oh good. Now that we got that straight. It works out great because they still call you for every possible age and number of siblings in a set. I will remind you, I am not a kid person but, give me a kid in need and I am your girl.

I will get fierce and fantastic for a person who needs help finding a voice. Game face is on and I am ready for battle. But that's not exactly how it works with foster care. No, you cannot take every kid or sibling set they call about. I had to get my brain around it.

The *saying Yes* part is a great first step when it comes to following God. When it gets hairy is when things seem to fall apart. Sometimes I thought I was all in, and I was, but it was not without massive struggles. I have made so many dumb decisions in life as a mom and otherwise.

We are hard on each other as moms. I have already touched on that. But as I was in my pocket serving my butt off for God, I made some radical screw-ups. I disconnected from my marriage. I drank way too much in more than one season of life. I spent too much money. Once I left a sleeping baby in my car while I went in and watched 30 minutes of another kid's gymnastics class, only to run into one of my social workers and have a total and complete freak out. I remember running to the car. The baby was still sleeping soundly.

I put my head on the steering wheel and lost my mind. I could have gone to jail. I could have messed up everything. I was serving but I was so tired. I forgot her. I totally forgot a helpless child in the car. Praise God, He protected all of us. So, when crazy stories happen involving parents and kids, I have a whole different view of it. I did it. It could have turned out awful. I could have been the foster mom on the Five O'clock News. Eek. I can promise you, as much as we want to judge another, we simply have no idea what they are going through or what brought them to the place they are in.

Jesus Knew What Was Up

I am about to preach this one from the mountaintops y'all. Remember in the Bible when the woman was about to be stoned to death? Holy crap. I am the woman on so many levels. If sin is sin is sin, maybe we all are that woman. Then, like a total rock star, Jesus pipes up and tells them to go ahead, anyone who has not sinned and throw the first stone.

That was the moment for a serious mic drop. Hello. Wake up, all ye humans. Man, Jesus had a way. Dang, you guys, they were going to stone a woman to death for her indiscretions. Are you fully getting this, my people? Can you even imagine what that must have been like for that woman in that moment? She must have been terrified. Then out of nowhere, there is Jesus with all of His perfect words.

Maybe I am preaching after all. How happy am I to live in this modern world? I would have been stoned to death for real back then. If you have never checked out this story you can find it in the New Testament, in John chapter eight. If you read the whole chapter, you will get all filled up with some serious conviction. I have thrown a stone or 100 in my day. God has brought me through a few deserts to help me realize I have no business judging others. And while I totally get it most days, that sinful nature of mine creeps in still.

Get Up on That Yes!

I have watched people I love as they begin to feel the weight of saying *yes*. Friends are lost, or in some cases let go. Things that we all thought would stay the same forever are dismantled. It's not for the faint of heart. I have listened to my friends tell stories of having a solid and happy life and one day God calls them to move their family across the U.S. away from all the people they love so dearly. Sometimes, the move is to Africa or Guatemala. The stories are so many and so similar.

I love to be around people who are right in the middle of their *yes*. They have a certain fire and passion that is not the norm. It is almost like you can see it in their eyes. Even though they may be tired and weary, they are certain. It is inspiring and magnetic and challenging to my soul. Which reminds me, right about now is a great time to take some inventory.

What does your circle look like? Are you surrounding yourselves with warriors and doers of the Word? Some of the most inspiring women I have encountered were nothing like me. We tend to flock toward similar personalities, but I am challenging you to expand yo' circle, girl.

It is easy to get comfortable. Maybe you have a group of awesome women who love the Lord. Good for you. How many of you are stepping out in faith and sharing it with one another? What does it look like? Who is inspiring you to dream bigger and live bolder? Occasionally, we need to be dumped out of our comfort zones. It is scary. I have been there more than once. Sometimes, even with the best intentions, we maybe get a little stale. Complacent. Comfortable. Predictable. It happens.

In my own life several years ago, I knew the tides were shifting in some of my relationships. We were all God loving mommas, but I had made my circle too small. I tend to be that girl. I can talk to a crowd like we are besties, but when it comes to having a big circle, it is work for me. I do great one on one, but when I get comfortable, my nature is to stick with the few I trust with my life.

God had other plans for me, however. He has been pushing me intensely to open my eyes and mind to what He has for me. My friend group has since become extremely diverse. It is not nearly as safe as it felt even a few years ago, but it is right. He has stuff to do in and through me, and most times I just need to get out of the way.

What is God Calling You To?

Maybe you know and are doing it and feeling the sting and the excitement. Maybe you have no clue but know it is time to dig in. Maybe He is asking you to do something that feels scary and you are hoping it will pass. I want to encourage you, my friend, it will be brilliant. God wants more for us than we can ever imagine. Yes, there is pain in the *Yes*, but there is also an astounding peace in knowing you are in the pocket. You can screw up. You can also pick up where you left off. I am with you. Actually, we all need to be with each other, gently nudging and totally encouraging one another to go big. Find one or two people and start the conversation. Hold each other accountable and never stop. This is what it is all about.

> I want to be obsessed with following God like my twelve-year-old is obsessed with slime.

I totally do not get the whole slime deal, but I know she loves it. It is totally her thing. And as grownups while life woos us with lots of shiny things, in the end they do not fill us up. We have this life, today. It is time we get to it. Girlfriends, Unite!

Get a sister in yo' corner! This is mine! She really is…all that!

CHAPTER 10

THE PURSUIT OF HAPPY-ISH

These girls get it.

Telling Fear to Stick It

I'm going out guns a-blazing. I don't want to look back at my life and think about what could have been. I think about my choices sometimes and I get a very sobering reminder what living all out looks like. When we pay bills every month for the four thousand things five daughters need and love, there is a reality check. Occasionally, I get overwhelmed. Right about the time I feel my chest start to tighten, I am reminded that God brought us into all of this chaos. I would not change it for the whole world. I have days where I am certain I will lose my mind trying to wrangle everyone and get all the humans where they need to go, but I do it. Extreme joy does not always look like the pick-up bus I drive on a daily basis. It is a bit like a hamster wheel.

Remember that movie Groundhog's Day? I can so relate. I figured it out the other day, I have been taking kids to school every day for six years. Every day I make the same loop, twice. It has grown to three drop offs currently, as we now have one big bad middle schooler on our hands. In two more years, we will have four drops in the morning and four pick-ups in the afternoon. So, I am going to work really hard until then to get my full Zen on. 'Cause Lord knows I am going to need it. And so, it goes. I am sure you have your own little version of whatever to mess with your brain.

Let me post the disclaimer before someone tells me how blessed I am to have these five children. I am blessed beyond measure. If my blessings were measured in tattoos, I would have a full body tat. But if you are reading this far, I am guessing you have figured out I kind of tell it like it is.

I struggle with my humanness and the day to day occasionally. In total, I will drive the pickup bus as I have labeled it since 2000, and I still have thirteen years of it ahead of me. Oh, sweet baby Jesus, help me. I will be a ripe age by the time I am finished. I can only imagine how much time I will have to hone my parenting skills during these many, many years to come. Maybe I will stop screaming completely. What if I overcome the evil eye I can give like no one else in the rearview mirror? Wow, I GET to learn so much. I am pumped. So, while I want my joy, dammit, I am sure to find it in my sticky kid-crusted suburban. I will be on the same route for over the next decade if you are ever trying to locate me.

If we want sanity, or in my case a small sliver of sanity fused with some oddities and a good pair of shoes, we must dig in to more happiness. What are some of the things that really just give you joy in your regular, everyday life? I am not talking about that one time you went to some expensive place and did expensive things 'cause those things are fleeting, y'all. Or maybe because I don't get to do them much, I am going to say they are fleeting, so I feel good about me. Either way....

Pure Joy Must-Haves

Here's what is on my punch-list for a happy life:

- *Coffee.* Do I even need to say anything more? I only learned about coffee a handful of years ago. Can you imagine? I am obsessed with keeping my coffee hot. So, I will add a little Yeti coffee cup to this part of my hallelujah list.

- *Sunshine.* You guys, living in the Midwest is not my spirit animal type situation. As I long to be a West Coast momma, I will settle for a sunny day with the top of the Jeep off, music blaring.

- *Laughing.* You guys, we must laugh more. There is never enough cackling. Always do more of this. And please, just as important, find friends who think you are funny. I happen to be on the inappropriate side as we have already had a one-sided discussion about. Find friends who get you instead of judging you for it. It will change everything. Also, I am an extremely loud laugher. When my sister and I get together, people stare because we have the exact same super loud cackle. So, if you and I become besties prepare for these awkward things about me.

- *Dance Parties.* There are never enough of these either. Make a few friends who like the stuff you like. I love to dance. I have friends who love to dance, and they make my life much fuller in the joy department. We go to each other's houses and dance our butts off by the pools as our kids look at us and roll their eyes. They have watched our dated dance moves for years and are seemingly unimpressed. We have since figured out the reason they respond this way…it is because they are so jealous of our moves. Duh.

- *My mom and sister.* If you are blessed enough to have a goldmine here, make them a priority. We are all so different and so happy together. Our lives and relationships have not been perfect, but we are always there for each other and when we do get the chance to be together, we are in full bliss mode.

Of course, I love Beck and my kids. They are amazing in all ways, but I am talking about what is outside our walls that help us feel basic, every day joy. We need to feel joy deep in our bones. We need outlets other than our immediate families to help fill our tank so we can return home and be our best version of our fabulous selves.

I will tell you living in a third world country has helped my perspective on joy. I think it was 2002 when I studied abroad in Thailand then went on to be in several countries in Africa. We have no real clue how our lives are gifted as Americans. Most of us will never have to worry if we can feed our kids or if we will have a safe place to lay our heads. Many of our thoughts of worry surround finances. I am in this boat also, so it is not like I have risen above it. But when I find myself in total stress mode, wondering how to plan ahead to pay for all the things all of these kids need for the next forever, I am gently reminded how much we have right here and right now. Once I realign, the fear tends to roll back out with the tide and there is a space for joy again.

Staking Our Claim

So how do we claim our stake in joy? I am not going back to allowing weeks to get past me. Nope. Not gonna happen. Have you seen the t-shirt that says, "Not Today Satan…Nope, Not Today"? Okay, something about the word Satan makes me think all pitchfork and red cape so I can't get the t-shirt because it just doesn't jive with me, but I like the concept! I have come to learn in a very massive way, there is an enemy who wants to keep us from experiencing joy. Ok, I might have lost a few of you there. Girls, I am sharing my experience. If you want to really dig in, do Priscilla Shirer's: The Armor of God Bible Study Book. [4] You will get all the right kind of info to seriously go to battle with God. And plus, hello, Priscilla is the stuff. God has used so many of her words to help heal my soul.

Average.

What a buzzkill of a word. Imagine if your parents were bragging on you as a kid, "She is average. What a gal. We love her so much in her sheer regular-ness."

No one wants to be average. I want to be a freaking renegade! We don't all have to be the same, that would make for such a boring world! But average is not one of the qualities I aspire to. The older I get, the less I care about fitting the mold. We have a tough role as women. There are magazines and TV shows, and social media and everything under the sun reminding us how far we are from looking like the ones so buxom and flawlessly represented. It is a lie, girls. It is a huge lie. It is time we call the bluff and change the future for ourselves and our sons and daughters.

So, let's say we are gonna go for it. You might be asking, *Where the heck do we even begin?* Or…*yeah, that sounds great, but you have no idea what goes through my head.* Actually, I bet I do.

One place we can start is by the people we surround ourselves with. There will always be a world out there we cannot measure up to. There will always be someone in the pickup line judging us. There will always be a drama, but only if we engage. We don't actually have to consider what others think about us. If we have a solid posse of truth tellers and our eyes are on God, even with our radical humanness, we are gonna do just fine.

Think about how much time you have spent in your life worried or considering what people will think about you. Oh my gosh, it makes my skin crawl just thinking about it. Will we ever be in a place to be completely free from it? I am not sure I have the ultimate answer to that question, but I do know I am in a season where slowly and surely, I am letting go. I started letting go years ago but this is a new level. Know this, if you are following God, people will not understand your ways. You will not blend in. You will stand out in whatever way He chooses. There is a reason for it. He is the reason for it.

All In

Are we willing to go there? Some days I am more than others. I had the best realization at coffee a few weeks ago with my girlfriends. After talking all kinds of fashion and kid challenges, my friend Jeri asked the question, "What would you do if you had no fear?"

Hold on. I was not caffeinated enough for that one. It took a second. I wanted to blow it off. It was too early in the morning to go so deep. It hit me hard though. I felt that familiar lump come up in my throat and out of nowhere, I wanted to bawl. So many things, that is what I would do. Sooo many things. Geez, I thought I was living free, but it was just another old soggy band-aid that got pulled off. I needed to hear this. This was divine intervention. Girls, that is why you have friends who are all things and friends you can be ridiculous with. You can laugh until your gut hurts, talk about completely superficial stuff and then cut completely to the chase of what makes life matter.

When my girl Jeri posed the question, it riled something up inside me. I almost felt mad, mad at myself mainly. I had gotten careful again. Pain causes us to shut down, play small, be careful. It generates fear. And we all know, fear is a total liar! Here's one thing that came out before the very deep stuff which God is still sorting out in my heart. "I would have a tattoo sleeve."

"Uh…huh?"

Followed by, "Why don't you do that? You do stuff that is clearly not normal. Why not do it? You are afraid of THAT?"

I guess I was. We have a professional business and I live in conservative, small town middle America. When I go to visit my sister in Austin, Texas, I feel as if I am in my true homeland. I feel like a fish out of water here though. I bet God likes that. He probably put me here for that exact reason.

So, I get to choose. I bet you can guess what I am working on right about now. We don't have to all be the same. We don't have to think the same or dress the same or even have the same opinions on tattoos. I am working my way to a new level of joy by just choosing to be me. The real actual ME not who I think I should be or who I think you might want me to be. The layers are peeling back as we speak.

- Who are you?
- Do you know?
- What are the things that are hidden deep within you?
- What are you terrified for people to know about you?

These are questions we have to answer on our journey to freedom. The things we have the most regret about also carry the most shame. I won't even go into shame because Brené Brown wrote the book on women and shame, literally.[5] And friends, we have a boat load of it. Shame intermingles with our fears and soon enough we are not even sure who we are anymore. I want to say this about our deep, dark secrets. I so hope I can get the right words out, or even if they are lame, God will use them and make them His.

Jesus, Take the Wheel

Our deepest, darkest secrets are stealing our lives.

We are so sure that we could never share our secrets. We push and shove them down and even as they bubble up, we use secondary things to distract us. Maybe it is alcohol, or porn (yes, I went there), or spending more money than we make, or even simple every day on the phone with your girlfriend gossip. They are stealing our lives. Horrible stuff happens. Some of it is a result of our poor decisions, and some of it we had zero control over. Either way it has become part of our story. We all have something we are trying to hide. Our pain and shame produce the fear and the fear paralyzes us. We begin to believe the lies. Maybe we have been playing those lies over and over in our heads for a lifetime.

Listen, the lies, the pain, our crap, as awful as we think they are, just might also be the key to our freedom if we face them. The power shifts when we decide it does. Did you get what I just said? The thing that has been holding us back for years could be the very thing, if shared, that could heal others. Hear me on this one. Your pain. My pain. I know it is so hard. It has defined us. But it doesn't have to. Facing it can open a door to a better life. As long as we live in our heads believing the lies, we actually believe it is the truth. Once the words are spoken in a safe place, the fear is slowly released and that is when the power can come. This is true joy, sisters; waging war on our fears.

My life has been a series of kicking and screaming and finally letting go, at least part of the time. I am not a pastor or a theologian or one of the important sounding Jesus-y kind of women, but I do have a story. I bet it is not much different than yours. The details might look dissimilar, but the journey is filled with a good deal of the same stuff. So, what if we look from this day forward and decide what we want. What will make your life have meaning? What will fill your hole that pain has created? And what are you going to do about it?

I can tell you from a boatload of personal experience the thing that must be a factor in changing your life is action. My husband and I own a clinic where people come for natural health solutions. When people show up, they think it is about losing weight. But it is about far more than they can imagine at the time. The results are great from a health standpoint, but the life change is what it is actually about. We need to connect with what has been missing or is missing in life and deal with pain to bring healing from our past.

Get Your Power Back

It is phenomenal to watch women get their power back. We spend our lives (especially as moms) doing and going and paying for all the things our kids want and need. Our lives slip away as we commit to too many things for too many people. We get lost. Many times, our clients tell us it has taken years to get brave enough to come into the clinic. They will spend hundreds and sometimes thousands of dollars on their kid's sports and desires, but they allow themselves to stagnate on the back burners.

It is not so different outside the doors of our clinic. The world is serving us lies and constantly putting Baby in the Corner. It doesn't have to be that way, but it has been. Similar to the women who come to our clinic, we must do something to change our current life situations. We must ACT. If we truly want joy, we have to go after it. No one is going to bring it to us. Guess what? No one is thinking about us. I mean, sure there might be that one person who loves to be in our business, but only because she is struggling with the same fears we are. We are the only ones who can actually change the world.

True world change starts within us. We are enough right where we are. We can be bruised and maybe broken and kind of messed up. So, what? Those are words.

Am I broken?

Hell, no.

I am a child of God. I am a daughter of the King, and don't you ever forget it!

You are too. Now go get your power! You have it right inside of you, begging to get out. Maybe you have been dying to live the way you feel on the inside, but still crave to have it match your outside.

Me too. Hence my tattoo journey. Maybe it is something else? Maybe you have this crazy gift that you don't believe would make any sense to pursue. Maybe you know you are supposed to speak up but haven't found your voice so far. Or maybe you were once powerful, and you lost it. Friend, you get a do over. If you don't have the power, ask for help. I have had friends carry me through seasons. I have had God carry me through life, even when I was not speaking to Him.

Palms Up

Take action! Do it today. Set your goal and roar like a freaking lion. Imagine how powerful you just might be. I am talking to you as much as I am to myself. It is not like I have already mastered these things. But I am working on it.

Joy. I will have it in spite of my circumstances. Some days I will bomb out and hit the McD's drive thru for a large fry and follow it up with a long nap when I should be productive. But, you better believe I will get back on that horse.

It has been quite a journey with God up to this point. I have done a good deal of running. I have shut Him out. He has been patient and sometimes fierce in dealing with me. I have also been all in, which is my current status. Even writing this book has been a huge *Yes*. Maybe tens or thousands of you will read it. Or, maybe I will force my kids to skim through it one day, but God was clear with me to *write*. In life, we want a big return. We see these phenomenal women of God who write and speak and just blow our doors off with inspiration. We have to remember they are regular girls like us. They decided one day to take a risk. I can also take a risk and see what happens. Sometimes our massive efforts are for one, and one is enough.

Saying *Yes* to God is an adventure. In the past eleven years most specifically, he has taken every single one of my *Yes* moments and changed my life in a way I would not even recognize if I would have taken a break and come back to myself. Wait, what? When did we decide to have five kids? Where did all those wrinkles come from? What have you done to yourself, woman? And why all the black leggings? For goodness sake, woman, WE LOVE FASHION! Get ahold of yourself!

> God has a plan we can't begin to wrap our heads around. I promise. Take it from me when I say He will lead you to places you would never in a thousand years imagine.

And with every *Yes* comes a new intimacy with Him. I still run sometimes, but as the nudges come, I am clear when He is calling me to do something. Some are big, and some are small, but they all add up to this life we are not expecting.

So, when I started praying with my palms up, "You can have it all, Lord," you better believe He showed up. From baby steps in high school when I recommitted my life every few months while I was just trying to figure it out, to big stuff. Colossal stuff. He is in it all. All the little *Yes* instances deposit in the faith bank. Then when He calls us to adopt a kid, or marry the guy, or take the job, we are a bit steadier. When pain and loss hit, we can feel Him sustaining us through it.

And when I was at my most lonely time in life and hanging on to God, I remember a fervent prayer, "I give it all to you, Lord. I don't want to live another second doing life without being all in."

He said, "I want you to give your kidney to a stranger…" But that is a story for a different day.

The road to putting my heart on my "sleeve" literally.

CONCLUSION
WOMAN UP

Those Mountains Won't Move Themselves

Oh friends, it has been fun. If you only knew the hurdles that popped up in my life right when I committed to write this book. God has to be so obvious with me in most cases. I had been feeling the nudge to write this book for some time. Within one day, I had three separate people tell me randomly they felt God leading them to tell me to write. (Hey, maybe that is how much God loves you.

Maybe it was all for you.) I remember going to the Catholic church to pray one day. It has become a haven for me and the Lord. I had a friend tell me many months ago the church was always open, and I didn't have to be Catholic to go in and pray any time. I decided to try it.

I was having a hard time getting quiet enough on my own. What God has done in those quiet times has literally changed my world and has given me the courage to press on in so many areas. The particular day I was there praying about this book, I had heard the same word from two people I loved and trusted, point taken. But I needed to hear from God. I asked so specifically for some massive signs. Knowing what I needed, God laid out the plan. By the end of the day, I had a woman I barely knew private message me with the exact message the other two people in my life had given me. Hours later I would turn on the TV to a show I had never watched before. In the middle of the night, no doubt, only to learn about a woman who was an author coach. What the heck. There was another sign.

I took action, because if God is sweet enough to indulge me and answer my prayer in such a massive way, I am moving. I have not stopped moving from that day. Hell and high water have come and gone and come again since then. Wouldn't it be sweet if I could say as soon as I said *Yes*, He cleared my schedule, so I could write? Nope. Quite the opposite. I couldn't write these words... only God. If it helps one woman or hundreds, it is worth it to be obedient for me.

I want to thank you for taking this healing journey with me. I feel somewhat exposed and equally relieved to be honest and real about my life in hopes it will give another hope. I also want to be your cheerleader. Not in the traditional sense, because I was a terrible cheerleader…like really bad, but it was a cute outfit on my teenage body. We need people who make us laugh, cheer us on, and kick our ever-loving butts when we need it. If you don't have these people, start praying for them and be willing to open your circle. I have found I have several circles now, which was odd for me at first.

Get on out of that comfort zone, girl! I wouldn't push you to do it if I wasn't doing it myself. Make friends with people who are not like you, be it race, culture, marital status, income level, or age. We all have something to offer each other and somehow our stories align, and we find we are more similar than different.

Go get this life. I hope you do it. I hope you rock the crap out of your time on this planet. I can't wait to hear your story of courage and overcoming. We are all overcomers. Give yourself grace and be gentle with yourself. Life will be hard enough. If you have a dream, make it a reality. Mess up. Failure ain't a thang. Trust me. Your story makes your life.

You are worth it. All of it. And don't be surprised by what God calls you to. It will most likely and certainly blow your mind in all the right ways.

From our girl power to yours!

Big Love,
Chantelle

OUR CHAOS

LENNIE

DOLLY

ARI

SOLIE

BIANCA

ABOUT THE AUTHOR

Chantelle Becking is an adoptive/foster momma to five, fab and fierce girls and is married to the world's most rad hubs (proven fact). She tells it like it is and has loads of love and screw-ups to share. She is a regular gal with a passion for fashion, a love for God and a questionable mouth.

Though God told her to write this book, Chantelle is not a NY Times Best Seller (yet). She is brutally honest and funny about her adventures running from and with God. Her mission is to share "the real" in hopes of helping you see that your not-so-shiny moments are fine and dandy, and there is no room in this mission field for shame. GIRL, GO BE! Get the freedom in stepping away from the filtered photos of the façade, realize there is no magic pill, sit in who you are, realize some days we win, some days we learn. Literally anything is possible if we dwell less and act more. Get about those dreams. They are just waiting for you.

Known as the inappropriate friend, Chantelle's motto is to always be your funny and quirky self. Through her transparency, you'll be inspired to let yo' freak flag fly and soak in the unfiltered day-to-day chaos of everyday life.

(P.S. – *This book already has rave reviews by at least five Becking daughters who are happy to use it as an in-home frisbee.*)

CONNECT WITH CHANTELLE

Let's face it…SHE IS EVERYWHERE!
Instagram @chantellebecking
Facebook @chantellebecking

Check out her shenanigans right here:
www.chantellebecking.com
for Booking Info,
Upcoming Speaking Events,
And Fun Stuff You Can Buy that is Rad.

DID YOU LOVE THIS BOOK?

Here are some ways you can help others connect to this life-changing message:

Write a Review

1. Go to amazon.com
2. Search for "*Unapologetically You*"
3. Click on "Write a Customer Review"
4. Rate the book (5 stars would be awesome) and write your review.

Share

Post a picture of you and the book on your social media and tag me!

Give

Buy one for a friend who needs to know she's doing a great job.

Thank you so much. You rock!

WORKS CITED

Chapter 2

[1] *The Bible.* New International Version. Retrieved from The Message Bible App: November 2018.

Chapter 7

[2] *The Bible.* New International Version. Retrieved from The Message Bible App: November 2018.

Chapter 9

[3] *The Bible.* New International Version. Retrieved from Biblehub: November 2018.

Chapter 10

[4] Shirer, Priscilla. *The Armor of God Bible Study Book.* Lifeway Christian Resources, 2015.

[5] Brown, Brené. *I thought it was just me: Women reclaiming power and courage in a culture of shame.* New York: Gotham, 2007.